Shared Trust in New Zealand –

**Strategies
for a
Small
Industrial
Country**

Martin
Perry

institute of policy studies

First printed in 2001

Institute of Policy Studies
Victoria University of Wellington
PO Box 600
Wellington
New Zealand

© Institute of Policy Studies

•

ISBN 0-908935-54-4

•

Editor: Ginny Sullivan
Design/Layout: Sharon Bowling
Cover Design: Jacob Sullivan

Printed by Milne Print Ltd, Wellington

• Contents

Foreword   v
Preface   vii

1 – Introduction   1
2 – Small Industrial Countries   9
3 – Business Systems and Small Country Differences   38
4 – Shared Trust in New Zealand   63
5 – Promoting Business Cooperation   78
6 – Conclusion and Recommendations   100

Appendix – List of Interviewees   117
References   119

• Foreword

Small, isolated countries share a number of economic disadvantages – most notably the lack of scale economies that larger countries can reap. While there are many intangible advantages from living in a small, isolated industrial country such as New Zealand, one would hope that there may also be some economic advantages that help to offset the disadvantages.

In this monograph, Martin Perry examines whether an often cited advantage for small countries – that of high degrees of shared trust across businesses enabling mutually beneficial co-operation – is as strong in New Zealand as it is in a number of other similar countries. He produces evidence of high levels of shared trust amongst businesses in the Nordic countries. In contrast, he finds relatively low levels of trust and co-operation amongst businesses in New Zealand. Perry analyses historical reasons as to why there is this paucity of shared trust amongst businesses in New Zealand and suggests potential paths forward to promote business co-operation.

The Institute of Policy Studies is pleased to have helped facilitate Martin Perry's research on this topic, hosting his visit to New Zealand and publishing the end result of his work. New Zealand's economic performance is an area of strong interest to the Institute and we hope this study – together with other related studies undertaken here and elsewhere – will ultimately prove fruitful in lifting this country's performance and living standards.

Arthur Grimes
Director
Institute of Policy Studies

• Preface

This investigation originates in work commenced when the author was an employee of the former New Zealand Institute for Social Research & Development (1992-94). The Institute undertook several investigations of attempts to promote business cooperation that led to the conclusion that there had been a peculiar reluctance within the business community to cooperate. A convincing explanation as to why that should be so was not immediately evident.

This present investigation seeks to offer such an explanation. It does so by comparing New Zealand with other small industrial economies. As well as filling an explanatory gap, the comparison is presented because there seems to have been little thought to the potential role model provided by other and typically more successful small industrial economies.

Perhaps because small industrial economies are predominantly European, they have been thought to be of little relevance to a comparatively remote nation in the South Pacific. This study seeks to correct such a perception and to encourage thinking about what it means to be a small industrial country.

While the writing of this study has been undertaken in my place of employment, the study would not have been possible without a period of study leave in New Zealand (November-December 1999). I am indebted to the Institute of Policy Studies for hosting me during that visit and to the National University of Singapore for granting me six weeks of study leave.

During that time I met with a large number of people working in government, other public agencies, industry associations and business management. I also completed a short questionnaire survey that obtained over 100 responses. I am grateful to all of those who provided me with information through either or, in some cases, both of these data collection mechanisms. In some cases my interviewees were re-visited after I first obtained their assistance in my earlier research. This ability to follow up on prior conclusions was particularly helpful, and I am especially grateful for the cooperation of all of those involved.

Finally, I would like to thank Trade New Zealand for financial support to the Institute of Policy Studies that made this publication possible and viii

the Treasury for commenting on an earlier draft. The support of these organisations does not imply any responsibility or endorsement of the views expressed.

Martin Perry
Department of Geography
National University of Singapore

1 • Introduction

It has become commonplace that New Zealand went through an economic revolution after 1984. There is some debate about whether the revolution was permanent or merely an experiment and whether it should be described as 'liberalisation' or merely 're-regulation'. Those debates aside, the broad consensus is that a radical departure in economic management and business organisation was enacted. It is difficult to dispute this in terms of the range of changes that was introduced in rapid quick-fire succession. This haste was possible because it was a state-led revolution. If the method rather than the content of the 'revolution' is considered, there is perhaps a greater element of continuity and consistency than that label implies. Government has been the agent of change since European colonial settlers first sought its protection and development support in the mid-nineteenth century. The post-1984 government-led change is sometimes accused of being different because it was not sanctioned by the electorate in advance. How significant that alleged aloofness from a democratic mandate is judged to be depends partly on what expectations are held about the appropriateness of other decision-making processes.

One contrast that can be drawn is with a system in which decision-making is shared between governments and organised interest groups, such as labour and employer associations. Such a tripartite, consensus-seeking approach was rejected by the Rogernomics revolutionaries on the grounds that it was unworkable and inconsistent with their purpose (Oliver, 1989). It was unworkable because interest groups had no authority over their membership. It was inconsistent because interest groups were regarded as protectionist lobbies unable to look beyond their narrow self-interest. The former was indisputable. The lack of authority held by interest groups has been the flip side of the long-standing dominance of the state. The self-seeking nature of interest groups is correct but not straightforward. The demands of interest groups vary according to their organisation and the environment in which they operate. Fragmentation of New Zealand's interest groups and the absence of encompassing 'peak' associations made them particularly unhelpful to economic modernisation. Earlier reform efforts had recognised that fewer, stronger interest groups may have been able to play a constructive role in economic development, but realising

1

such reorganisation had challenged policy-makers. Hence, the lobby in favour of proceeding through consensus was not strong and those who advocated leadership 'from the top' could point to the past ineffectiveness of earlier attempts at joint decision-making.

A second aspect of continuity can be seen if the consequences of the 'revolution' are considered. The direct influence of the state has reduced over many aspects of business activity and economic management. Continuity exists in the absence of any compensatory growth of organised, encompassing interest groups with the possible exception of the Business Roundtable and its representation of corporate business. In respect of labour groups, this is quite understandable. Legislative change reduced the organisational capacity of trade unions. It may be considered more of a puzzle that the withdrawal of the state from many aspects of business regulation has not resulted in any greater organisation of business, in the sense of their participation in industry associations. The weakness and fragmentation of interest groups has been an enduring feature of the 'New Zealand business system'.

The suggestion that New Zealand has a business system is rather foreign to most recent debate about the country's development challenges. By comparison with Nordic corporatism, Japanese keiretsu capitalism or Chinese business networks, it might be thought that there is little that is distinctive about the organisation of business in New Zealand. This view has been encouraged by the emphasis on deregulation since the 1980s, which has contrasted a legacy of regulation and state intervention with the conversion to a 'free market'. Rather than being a product of distinctive challenges and institutions, the past resort to regulation and protection is presented as a failed distortion whose imprint can be erased as 'normal' market relations take shape. Comparison with other small industrial countries encourages greater attention to the origins and legacy of past intervention. Faced with similar development challenges, Europe's small industrial economies typically adopted corporatist modes of organisation that have failed to take root in New Zealand. Understanding the origins of this difference and the legacy created by alternative political arrangements points us to the distinctive contours of the New Zealand business system.

It is this contrast between New Zealand and other small industrial countries, particularly the high income Nordic small economies (Denmark, Iceland, Finland, Norway and Sweden), that provides the central theme of this investigation. Despite many differences of location, culture and economic specialisation, it will be argued that the challenges faced by small industrial economies are sufficiently common that it is meaningful to compare their development strategies. Assuming that this commonality is accepted, identification of how New Zealand has deviated from other small industrial economies has a three-fold relevance:

• It diversifies the debate about economic management away from a narrow focus on the appropriate relationship between government and business to include discussion about business organisation and behaviour.

• It can offer some resolution to the differing perspectives about the justification for reduced industry protection and welfare provision by noting how past intervention deviated from the pattern found in the high income small economies.

• It can point to new development agendas working within the parameters set by the reduction of border protection and limited direct government participation in industry development.

More particularly, the comparison with other small industrial economies draws attention to the potential influence of interest group organisation and business cooperation on industry development. In a small business community, individual participants have a comparatively high stake in their industry and these participants are much more likely to share common values and be personally known to each other than in the case of a large community. These conditions can facilitate an unusual degree of integration in a small business community exposed to international competition. In the Nordic economies, it has recently been claimed that this has occurred and that it has been the origin of much of their industrial success (Maskell et al, 1998). In comparison, the New Zealand business system has generally failed to capture the benefits of the cooperation that ought to exist in small economies. Understanding why this outcome has eventuated, the extent to which this has weakened industrial development and how the potential for business cooperation in a small country might be encouraged are the central concerns of this investigation.

At the outset, some commonly held perceptions about business cooperation in New Zealand warrant comment as they may cloud the acceptance of other possibilities. The importance of producer cooperatives in the agricultural sector might be pointed to as evidence of an inclination to cooperation. Such an interpretation overlooks that the purpose of an agricultural cooperative is first to ensure that farmer rather than industrial interests control the processing chain. In New Zealand, farmers have been motivated to protect the viability of the family farm against the imposition of industrial-style farming that outside control of processing and marketing would have imposed (Curtis, 1993). Once established, cooperatives consolidated ownership in pursuit of market domination with a greater aggression than private companies might have displayed (Brooking, 1992, p 239). The preponderance of interlocking directorships is another possible indicator of business cooperation that has attracted comment (Fogelberg and Laurent, 1973; Firth, 1987). The use, if any, that was made of the overlapping directorships has never been firmly established but it is likely that their significance was as a social network and system for patronage more than to promote business cooperation (Jesson, 1979, 1999).

Across society a tendency to participate in organised groups has been strong. From an early stage in the country's European settlement, a spirit of organisation has pervaded all spheres of life: public and private, business and leisure, family and club (Olssen, 1992, p 262). But the significance of this participation was not always as it seemed. Trade union membership was high, for example, but actual commitment and support low (Mabbett, 1995). Episodes of sharp social conflict have contrasted with the widely-held perception that inequality was low and everyone had a stake in 'God's Own' society, even when the reality was less sanguine (Gould, 1982).

Recent years have seen a growing number of business network groups such as those organised by Chambers of Commerce. These again could be seen as evidence of business interest in cooperation, but the reality is otherwise. A study of the networks organised by the Wellington Chamber of Commerce and Christchurch City Council concluded that members use such networks to market their own business and that they had little impact in promoting informal or formal forms of business cooperation (Field et al, 1994). In summary, many of the aspects of New Zealand business and society that have been viewed as cooperative have either operated differently than sometimes thought or have not been significant to development.

Comparison with other small industrial countries is made to substantiate the conclusion that New Zealand has been an 'uncooperative' economy. This part of the investigation will highlight the comparison between New Zealand and the Nordic economies . That focus is partly for practical reasons. Within the literature on small industrial economies, the experience of Nordic countries has attracted most attention, including the recent investigation referred to above (Maskell et al, 1998) and a recent comparison of trade, employment and welfare policies in Sweden and New Zealand (Mabbett, 1995). As well, the Nordic experience is of special interest because of their sustained high incomes and because, as well as size, they share with New Zealand a common origin as resource-based economies. A difference is the greater Nordic success in diversifying down the commodity-processing chain and in building high value-adding industries through networks of small businesses working in cooperative alliances.

Explanations of Nordic industrial strength have given prominence to business cooperation as a source of their industrial strength. That argument was made originally in connection with their corporatist style of political management. This explained Nordic success by reference to domestic political arrangements, such as tripartite bargaining institutions and proportional representation voting systems, that generated 'low voltage' politics and a willingness to share the costs of economic change. The result, it has been argued, was an unusual degree of community cohesion that enabled an open economy to be maintained in the face of international market instability. As subsequent chapters comment, the contribution of corporatist political management to Nordic economic success is complex. It may have imposed fewer burdens than New Zealand's use of trade protection but it similarly proved ultimately unable to sustain employment growth. As well, in today's increasingly integrated world economy some of the aspects of Nordic economic management that once made these countries distinctive have broken down or become less effective. Nonetheless, Nordic researchers continue to stress how business cooperation has remained an aspect of their industrial strength. The argument recently made is that Nordic business cooperation originates in the high degree of personal familiarity amongst business managers in a small economy. The continuing references to cooperation in Nordic economic success have encouraged this study to compare the conditions influencing business cooperation in New Zealand and the Nordic region.

The Argument in Summary
The starting point for this investigation is that smallness is a defining characteristic of New Zealand's development experience. Smallness, more

so than a colonial heritage or dependence on primary production, provides a base from which to examine the country's comparative economic performance. This perspective is sustained by identification of the common challenges faced by all small countries, namely their high exposure to international competition and their dependence on low-to-medium technology sectors. Smallness increases vulnerability to economic shocks, and is a disadvantage in the viability of high-tech industries, but it may have advantages in sustaining 'shared trust'. This quality facilitates cooperation within industries in ways that can assist innovation and help small industrial countries withstand market instability.

Given common characteristics, there is merit in comparing the institutional characteristics and development experiences of small industrial countries. The comparison between New Zealand and the Nordic economies is focused upon for three reasons: (i) Nordic economic success; (ii) the existence of prior investigation to draw upon; (iii) a common heritage as resource processing economies providing similarities other than size. The comparison reveals the following:

- The established account of New Zealand's exceptionalism amongst small countries has emphasised its divergence from the corporatist management and trade openness that has existed amongst Nordic and other small European states. This view needs to be updated. Corporatist arrangements have not enabled the degree of economic adjustment claimed (although they may have brought other benefits) and they have been weakened by the growing integration of national economies. Differences in trade openness have reduced with New Zealand's change in economic management.

- The origins of Nordic corporatism reveal a contrasting institutional history that has resulted in encompassing interest groups (employers and labour) and the maintenance of a high degree of communal authority (a sense of national interest). This legacy is suggested to explain the participation in industry associations that is a continuing characteristic of Nordic economies. As well, it has encouraged business specialisation. That attribute is a further inducement to business cooperation. New Zealand's institutional history has emphasised government rather than self-management as in the corporatist model. This has resulted in weak and fragmented interest groups and less stimulus to business cooperation than in Nordic countries.

- Nordic claims about the presence of shared trust in small economies have credibility in the context of the larger environment that supports business cooperation. With its different institutional inheritance, it is questionable that shared trust exists in New Zealand. This may identify a gap holding back industry development.

- Surveys of selected business managers and promoters/coordinators of business cooperation in New Zealand suggest that shared trust, as depicted in Nordic research, does not exist. As expected, there is personal familiarity and common values amongst managers but the business culture is judged uncooperative. Most respondents agree that attitudes to cooperation lag behind the potential benefits.

- The survey evidence is generally supported from the outcomes of past public policy efforts to promote business cooperation. The most successful of these initiatives has been Trade New Zealand's support to joint action groups but, with a few exceptions, the resulting groups have been difficult to sustain or develop. Even so, several reasons suggest that the best prospects for promoting business cooperation lie in support to industry groups. Alternative approaches that have or are being tried (support to 'hard networks' and business clusters) are based on unrealistic assumptions of business behaviour and competitive advantage. Encouraging participation in industry associations leaves individual managers free to determine the forms of cooperation that suit their needs. External support for industry associations may be justified from the barriers in obtaining participation.

These arguments commence in the next chapter by making the case for small industrial countries as a distinctive development category with respect to their economic challenges and the characteristic responses that have been made to those challenges. Chapter 3 explains the origins of New Zealand's exceptionalism as a small industrial country compared with those in Europe. This part of the discussion utilises business system theory to explain how the contrasting political contexts of the Nordic and New Zealand economies connect with their differences in business organisation and behaviour. Chapter 4 reports the findings of an original survey that offers a preliminary assessment of the state of 'shared trust' in New Zealand. Shared trust is a quality that, as explained in chapter 2, is thought to offer particular advantages to small industrial economies. Chapter 5 provides

8 • Shared Trust in New Zealand

further reflection on the state of business cooperation by discussion of recent initiatives to promote cooperation, drawing particularly on the role of Trade New Zealand in various forms of network promotion. Chapter 6 concludes the investigation and offers recommendations designed to assist the strengthening of industry associations.

2 • Small Industrial Countries

What kind of country is New Zealand? This chapter argues that smallness is the single most important attribute shaping economic development opportunities and challenges. Traditionally other aspects of New Zealand have been stressed to draw attention to its special development challenges. One view has emphasised the legacy of its being a former Dominion of the British Empire. Economic and political dependence on the British Empire, it is suggested, resulted in an economic specialisation that primarily served British rather than New Zealand interests and that resulted in an enduring vulnerability through the focus on commodity exports. Primary sector dependence is the second and related defining trait that has been claimed. This dependence, it is argued, has resulted in particular problems of economic management because of the instability of agricultural prices and the difficulty of obtaining market access given that overseas governments tend to protect their own producers from imports. There are merits in both arguments but also reasons why they provide only limited insight into New Zealand's distinctiveness.

The emphasis on the colonial legacy tends to assume that in some way the country would have been better off – richer, more industrialised and less vulnerable – if it had not been a British Dominion. This claim needs to be judged against the possible development options that might have been open to the country in the nineteenth century. Whatever the political status, assuming a desire for economic growth, the small internal market would have forced a focus on exports, and the limited indigenous supplies of labour and capital would still have required that resources be sought from overseas (Castles, 1988, p 40). Without a colonial link some form of similar connection to an export market might well have been deemed necessary to obtain influence in overseas markets. The focus on agricultural exports reflected the selection of activities of greatest comparative advantage within prevailing technologies and market opportunities rather than being imposed on unwilling suppliers. The British connection did impose constraints, as in the late 1930s when British financiers sought to favour investment in export capacity over social expenditure (Gustafson, 1986).

9

After the war, the commitment to long-term contracts for the supply of food to Britain reduced income from agricultural produce compared with what might have been obtained from open market sales (Mabbett, 1995, p 119). On the other hand, given that commodity markets were booming even without the British association, the rural sector would have retained its importance.

The case for agricultural specialisation as the country's defining characteristic is challenged by the fact that primary sector activities have played a declining role in the domestic economy since the 1920s (Brooking, 1992). Not until the 1950s did New Zealand's share of total employment directly employed in agriculture exceed that of Sweden, although Swedish agriculture had ceased to be a competitive export sector by the end of the nineteenth century from when it was sustained by trade protection (Mabbett, 1995, p 60). In New Zealand, an agricultural specialisation has remained, with problems from the declining terms of trade, but arguably the development issue to be explained is why a productive primary sector was not combined with a competitive manufacturing sector. Other industrial economies have managed to achieve such a combination, notably Denmark and Finland (Marceau, 1992).

As well as colonialism and a primary sector specialisation, the comparative geographical isolation of New Zealand is sometimes viewed as a distinctive challenge to industrial change. But isolation is a two-way street and distance has been a source of protection for manufacturing as well as an impediment to growth. Even today an industry such as furniture survives in New Zealand partly through the way that the costs of distribution favour local production. More generally, modern communications have greatly reduced the cost of distance and facilitated international exchange. Other aspects of distance such as the remoteness from sources of expertise or large markets are a potential challenge to all small countries, irrespective of their geographical location. Rather than isolation, the impact of location on the choice and character of trading partners has perhaps been of greater significance. Small countries neighbouring other small countries, for example, may have had an advantage over small countries bordering large countries. Nordic experience has been interpreted as showing that trade amongst small countries accelerates industrialisation and lessens reliance on commodity exports more rapidly than where the dominate trading relationship is with a large country (Walsh, 1988, p 41). This might be seen in New Zealand's trading history with Britain. On the other hand, Australia, another small country, has also been an important trading partner. As well, today it might be argued that geography is assisting New Zealand through comparative proximity to the fast-growing Pacific Rim.

All small industrial economies – advanced OECD nations with fewer than 25 million inhabitants[1] – are challenged by their tendency to be heavily reliant on export markets and a comparatively narrow range of export products. Vulnerability arising from a dependence on international trade is thus not uniquely a product of primary sector dependence, although the latter may accentuate vulnerability. Similarly, all small industrial countries are generally unable to sustain participation in new technology industries. This further underlines how the economic circumstances of small countries can make them more potentially vulnerable than larger ones. Overall, small industrial countries seem to have managed this vulnerability successfully, as indicated by comparatively high incomes per capita. Of course, there are exceptions reflecting how economic vulnerability is affected by variables other than size. Looking at Europe's small industrial countries, two explanations have been suggested for their high incomes. One has been corporatist politics because of the way this style of economic management sustained a collective response to external shocks (Katzenstein, 1985; Castles, 1989). The other explanation, developed in the context of the Nordic economies, has been that small economies benefit from 'shared trust' (Maskell et al, 1998). Shared trust refers to the potential capacity of small industrial countries to sustain unusually high degrees of inter-organisational cooperation, partly because of the uniform culture and density of personal contact networks in a small country.

Open Economies

Economists generally recognise that the smaller the country the more it needs to depend on others for goods and services and for its markets (Walsh, 1988; de la Mothe and Pasquet, 1996). Thinking of extreme cases, this relationship is bound to exist. A country that encompasses the globe would be self-sufficient; a small state is likely to have resource dependencies on others. The precise reliance on international trade might vary amongst small states, but there are some powerful reasons as to why declining size should encourage the opening of borders to world trade. It may maximise access to inputs and markets, assist economies of scale in the production of goods and intangible resources such as knowledge, help to curb domestic monopolies, help develop product differentiation and enhance overall industrial competitiveness through international exposure to best practice (Maskell et al, 1998, p 76). The increasing trend towards economies of scale and greater standardisation of products has tended to accentuate these imperatives by increasing the need for larger markets in many industries than the domestic economies of small economies can provide. As well, since large countries can sustain retaliatory action against small-country market protection longer and more effectively than could a small against a large country of similar income level, political realism promotes openness in small economies (McCann, 1995).

Small OECD countries[2] tend to have a higher degree of trade openness and exposure than medium and large countries (Table 2.1). The openness of economies in small countries (measured by the ratio of exports and imports to industrial production) is around three times that of large countries and a third higher than that of medium-sized countries. This pattern is consistent across all small industrial economies with the exception of Australia. The pronounced openness of the Nordic economies has developed since the 1970s, but for other European small industrial economies it is a longer established attribute (Castles, 1988, p 42). New Zealand remains somewhat of a laggard in its openness compared with other small industrial countries, although the extent of this difference was not always as great as popular opinion might suggest. In 1978, New Zealand's openness index was 63, close to the then prevailing Nordic average of 69 (OECD, 1998).

Another way of demonstrating the potential vulnerability of small industrial economies is through their exposure. The exposure of small countries (the share of output 'exposed' to international competition, which is taken as all exports plus domestic sales to the same proportion as the import penetration of the market) is almost three times greater than that of large countries (Table 2.1). Once again New Zealand is below the small country average but still much above the exposure of large countries and above that of medium-sized countries. Australia is unusual amongst small countries in having an exposure rating that is below the average score of medium-sized countries.

Openness and exposure have required that governments of small countries devote special efforts to managing their balance of trade and the potential instability of their domestic economy. The extent of real economic

Table 2.1 Trade Openness and Exposure by Country Size

	1978		1996	
Country group[1]	Openness[2]	Exposure[3]	Openness	Exposure
Small countries:				
– Nordic	69.26	57.54	90.69[4]	72.06
– All non-Nordic	72.67	59.00	85.78	79.29
– New Zealand	63.00	53.36	78.43[5]	61.53
– Australia	37.39	45.83	56.50	45.11
– All small	71.83	58.65	87.05	77.58
Medium-sized countries	—	—	63.72	54.53
Large countries	—	—	28.16	26.04

Notes:

1. Large countries = United States and Japan; medium-sized countries = Germany, UK, Italy, France, Spain; small countries = Canada, Australia Netherlands, Belgium, Portugal, Greece, Austria, New Zealand + Nordic countries (Sweden, Denmark, Finland, Norway, Iceland).
2. Openness = (export + import)/manufacturing production.
3. Exposure = [(export/production) + (1 - export/production x imports/ (production - exports + imports))] x 100.
4. Iceland 1995, other countries 1996.
5. 1995.

Source: Calculated from OECD STAN Database, 1998.

vulnerability indicated by high exposure rankings can vary. As noted above (p 10), Nordic openness may have been helped by their regional clustering and cross-border trade. The extent of foreign ownership and control of industry has also affected vulnerability. Countries of settlement with a heavy emphasis on capital intensive primary and extractive industries, such as Australia and Canada, have traditionally been dependent on the import of foreign capital. In the past, this has accentuated the impact of an international trade crisis by reducing access to capital and prolonging recession (Castles, 1988, p 47). On the other hand, the vulnerability of a small country is reduced by having significant numbers of home-grown multinational companies (Walsh, 1988, p 55). The structure of trade and investment flows is important as well as openness and exposure. An economy with a large internal market may be heavily dependent on the import of vital raw materials and may experience serious dislocation if price levels rise. Heavy dependence on a narrow range of exports is a potential problem for any economy although, once again, small economies are likely to be most at risk.

Low Technology

A small country reliance on low tech industries is revealed when technology intensiveness is measured by the ratio of the value of R&D expenditure to output, as per OECD definitions. When examined in terms of export dependency, small countries are almost three times more dependent on low tech industries than large countries (Table 2.2). Including both high and medium-high technology products, small countries are also behind medium-sized countries in the technology-intensiveness of their exports. Moreover, it is only in the mid-1990s that the Nordic small economies have matched the share of high technology exports achieved by medium-sized countries. Most small economies still lag behind larger economies, and for all small economies the gap with large countries has grown since the late 1970s (Figure 2.1). Conversely, both the Nordic and other small economies have retained a dependence on low technology exports well above that of both medium and large countries (Figure 2.2). The low participation in high technology amongst small countries is equally evident when measured as a proportion of national output (Maskell et al, 1998, pp 78-79).

A few small countries sustain a share of exports in high technology that exceeds the average of medium-sized countries, notably Sweden, Netherlands and Finland. These countries exceed the average high-tech export dependency for small countries and account for a large share of all small country high tech exports (Table 2.3). Ireland is another exception but only as a consequence of foreign investment. The high proportion of exports from high tech sectors does not reflect the nature of the activity in Ireland where the affiliates of foreign-owned organisations are primarily engaged in comparatively routine operations (Coe, 1997). As a share of GDP, Ireland's expenditure on R&D in 1996 was below 1.5%, only marginally above New Zealand (OECD, 1999).

Table 2.2 Technology Intensiveness of Exports by Country Type (1996)

	Technology intensity of exports (%)[1]			
Country group[2]	High	Medium high	Medium low	Low
Small countries:				
– Nordic	15.1	36.1	11.6	37.2
– All non-Nordic	11.6	40.2	13.6	34.6
– New Zealand	3.3	13.4	9.0	74.3
– All small	12.5	39.2	13.1	35.2
Medium-sized countries	14.0	49.8	13.0	23.2
Large countries	25.4	51.8	9.8	13.0

Notes:

1. Based on OECD definitions using R&D as a proportion of total production cost: high technology industries have R&D expenditure of 6% or more of total production costs; medium high technology 3-6%; medium low technology 1-2% and low technology less than 1%. Industries classified as high technology include aerospace, computers and office machinery, electronics, communications and pharmaceuticals. Low technology industries include petroleum refining, ferrous metals, paper and printing, textiles and clothing, wood and furniture, food, tobacco and beverages.
2. Definitions as per Table 2.1.

Source: Calculated from OECD STAN Database, 1998.

Sweden is a country with a large expenditure on R&D, at close to 4% of GDP in 1996, the highest amongst OECD countries. This includes a significant private sector component concentrated in a small group of large engineering and pharmaceutical companies. In 1995, the chemicals and fabricated metals and machinery sectors contributed over 80% of all business R&D expenditure (OECD, 1999). The Swedish case is special partly because its commitment to military neutrality has extended to the retention of indigenous military technology that has promoted the country's

Figure 2.1 High Techology Exports 1978-1996

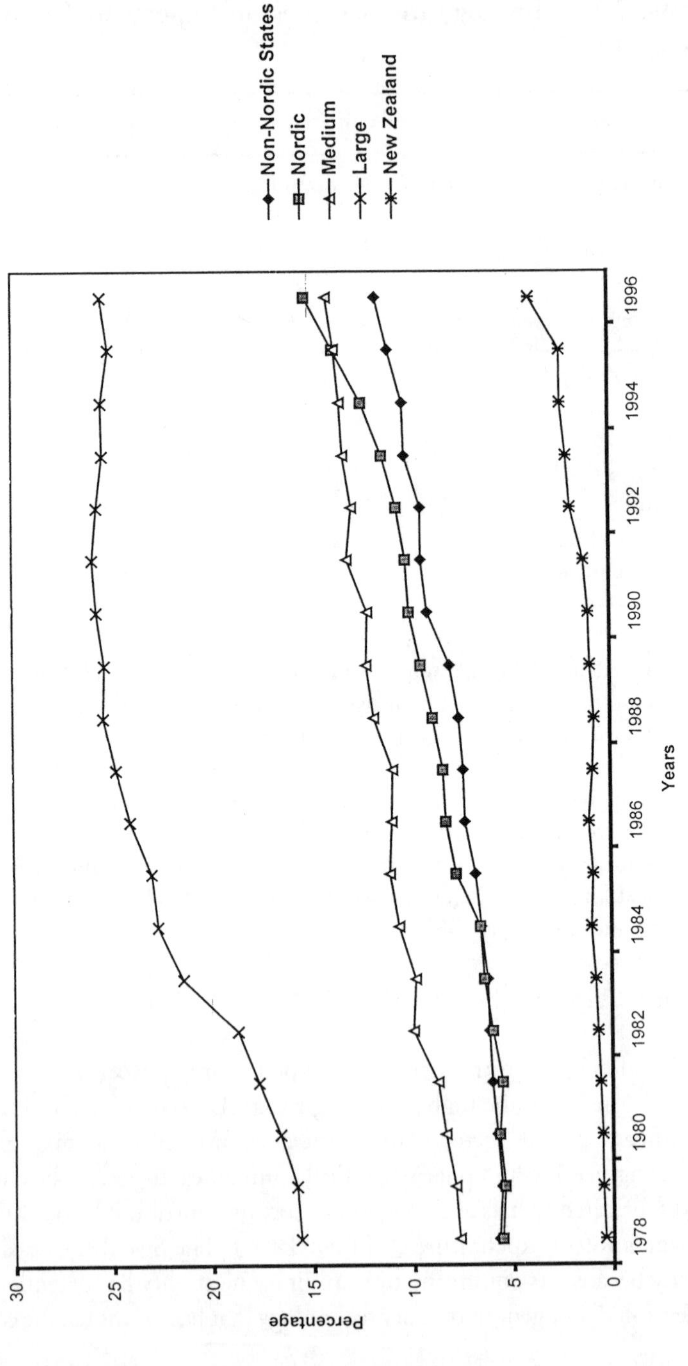

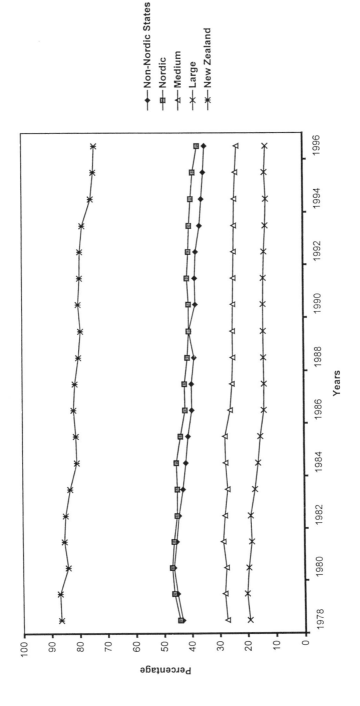

Figure 2.2 Low Technology Exports 1978-1996

participation in high technology. Doubts have been expressed about its capacity to sustain its defence industry, especially the aeronautics sector, which accounts for the source of much of the country's high tech capacity. Across Swedish industry as a whole, it has been judged that business has been slow in absorbing the results of R&D (Edquist and Lundvall, 1993, p 287).

The Netherlands, like Sweden, has sustained high technology activity amongst a small group of multinational companies. Their competitiveness against big country multinationals has been challenged with the shift to microelectronics that has been transforming the product markets served by Dutch multinationals (van Tulder, 1988). Finland is a more recent participant in high technology exporting. High technology in Finland is dominated by one company (Nokia) and mobile telephones. Communications equipment comprised 79% of Finnish high tech exports in 1996, and was the major contributor to the doubling of the share of national exports accounted for by high tech products since 1990 (OECD, 1999). In 1997, communications equipment accounted for 40% of all business R&D expenditure in Finland (OECD, 1999). Nokia's success as a mobile telephone equipment manufacturer partly reflects attributes of this industry that are not common in other high tech activities (Maskell et al, 1998). Amongst these unique characteristics are:

(i)   the continuity between modern digital technology and older electro-mechanical technology, whereas a strong break between old and new technologies is more typical of other electronics industries;

(ii)   ability to survive on the basis of standard components sourced from off-the-shelf suppliers;

(iii) the need to diversify usage in a small economy being a stimulus to design innovation ahead of producers in large economies;

(iv)   Nordic countries being favoured by the initial technological limitations of mobile telephones which most suited low density dispersed populations;

(v)   the influence gained over the design of industry standards through the early participation in mobile communication systems. Even so it was not until 1993 that Nokia earned significant profits, partly reflecting how its earlier investments in high tech projects such as computer manufacture had been unsuccessful (Dalum et al, 1988).

Table 2.3 High Technology Exports by Small Countries (1996)

	Share (%) national exports	Country share (%) of all Nordic or other small country high tech exports
Nordic		
Denmark	12.9	20.0
Finland	14.8	20.3
Iceland	3.8	0.2
Norway	5.8	4.9
Sweden	19.5	54.6
Other small		
Australia	10.9	4.8
Austria	9.6	8.0
Belgium	8.0	18.1
Canada	10.7	24.1
Greece	2.6	0.3
Netherlands	19.2	42.0
New Zealand	3.9	0.7
Portugal	5.6	1.9

Source: Calculated from OECD STAN Database, 1998.

20 • Shared Trust in New Zealand

The general pattern remains that maintaining a presence in high technology activities is much harder for small than larger countries. The impediments to high technology in small countries are numerous:

1. Small countries have more limited resources for R&D than large countries, but the variety of possible disciplines, projects and industrial sectors is not necessarily smaller (Walsh, 1988, p 42). R&D expenditure by the largest individual corporations exceeds the collective expenditure of individual small countries. New Zealand, for example, currently has an annual expenditure on R&D of around $900 million, which is around 11% of the annual R&D expenditure of IBM (Cookson, 1998). As well, the limited availability of venture capital constrains business from taking risks with new technology. The options for small countries are to spread resources thinly on select priorities. A further problem is that new technology development is frequently associated with innovation breakthroughs that result in the sudden devaluation of previous investment. A small economy has modest capacity to absorb such shocks (see Bray and Perry, 1994, for New Zealand case studies of this). Loss of skilled researchers to larger countries, where the resources and status allocated to their discipline are greater, means that it is relatively easy for large countries to acquire the results of small country research. Similarly, as many of the benefits from technology investment are captured in activities outside the original sector of application, obtaining a return on investment is harder in a small country than a large where there is more chance that the 'spill over' will be retained within the domestic economy. For a small country, to invest a lot in R&D has been likened to fertilising a field on a windy day: the neighbours benefit most (Maskell et al, 1998, p 87).

2. In the context of limited resources, the distribution of research effort in a small industrial country can be unhelpful to its needs. Basic science is cheaper than applied R&D and has attracted a disproportionate share of small country expenditure. For example, in the 1990s over a quarter of all R&D expenditure in Australia was on basic research compared with 16% in the USA (the same proportion as Norway) (OECD, 1999).[3] The absence of national research groups of significant size encourages researchers to orientate their work to the international scientific community. Per head of

population, New Zealand, Norway, Austria, Netherlands, Finland, Denmark, Sweden and Switzerland all exceed the rate of scientific publication across OECD countries as a whole (OECD, 1999). Researchers in a small country are often keener to publish theoretical papers abroad than apply their knowledge at home (Walsh, 1988, p 44). Large countries set research fashions and trends which small countries follow even, it seems, where the research topics are not necessarily relevant to their needs (Green, 1985).

3.   Innovation is an interactive and iterative process in which linkages to suppliers and users of the technology under development are critical for success (Fagerberg, 1995; Malecki, 1997). Business organisations in small countries tend to have less capacity to make use of leading edge technology than do those in large countries (Walsh, 1988, p 48; Edquist and Lundvall, 1993). The presence of advanced domestic users thus acts to reinforce large country advantage. Similarly there tends to be a continuing time lag between the availability of new technology in large and small countries (Maskell et al, 1998, p 88). Globalisation has accelerated the flow of resources mainly through the growth of multinational enterprise (Dicken, 1998). Large-country multinationals tend to retain a strong home-country bias that creates a time lag in the diffusion of new technology to subsidiary locations. Small-country multinationals, on the other hand, tend eventually to shift their technology development resources to centres of expertise in larger countries (Walsh, 1988, p 55; Edquist and Lundvall, 1993).

For small countries, one response to the technology challenge is to work cooperatively with other small countries (Walsh, 1988). The success of the Nordic economies in telecommunications has partly come about through such cooperation. In 1969 the Nordic public telecom administrations agreed to develop a common mobile phone system, which became the Nordic Mobile Telephone (NMT) system (Maskell et al, 1998, p 160). This responded to long-standing interest in mobile telecommunications arising from the needs of their geographically dispersed and sometimes remote populations. The development of NMT has been seen as a key event in the Nordic countries' success in mobile telecommunications. It provided a strong domestic market before the use of mobile telephones became widespread in large countries. It influenced the technology standards subsequently taken up around the world,

Table 2.4 Small Country Performance (1960-1997)

| | | GDP per capita | |
	Growth 1960-1997 (%)	1997 US$	Value added per employee 1996US$
Small countries:			
– Nordic	151	29,447	62,709
– Non Nordic	155	18,610	55,033
– New Zealand	60	13,974	42,861[1]
– All small	153	19,828	56,815
Medium-sized countries	153	20,169	58,346
Large countries	159	25,379	72,424

Notes:
1.   1995.

Source: Calculated from OECD STAN Database, 1998.

providing Nordic companies that had supported NMT with a long-term advantage. Small countries can, as this experience shows, find ways of competing in new technology but it does not alter the general position that small economies rely most heavily on low technology sectors. New Zealand is an extreme example of this, suggesting that some upgrading of its technology capacity is appropriate but within the limits of what is realistic for a small country.

Small Country Squeeze

A potential 'squeeze' on the viability of small industrial economies has been speculated on since the 1970s. Originally it was suggested that the growth of trade from large countries was a potential threat to the viability of small countries, given their high dependency on foreign markets (Kristensen and Levinsen cited in Walsh, 1988, p 38). More recently the risk of a dual squeeze on small countries has been perceived (Maskell et al, 1998). On the one hand, structural impediments mean that small countries must leave participation in high technology industry to large countries. On the other hand, sustaining a presence in medium and low technology sectors is challenged by the growing cost competitiveness of Asian and other new industrial economies.

Measured by GDP per capita, the extent to which the 'squeeze' has affected small industrial countries appears to vary. As a group, GDP per capita has kept pace with medium-sized countries, but in respect of current income the Nordic small countries exceed all others (Table 2.4). How significant the economic achievements of the small economies are judged to be depends partly on how tight the squeeze is perceived to have been. Being excluded from R&D, intensive industries can be less disadvantageous than often imagined (Grupp, 1995). Similarly, the growth of newly industrialising economies has impacted on industries such as consumer electronics but these have not been notable specialisations of small industrial countries, although some have tried to participate in them (Dalum et al, 1988).

The limited size of the national knowledge and capital base has encouraged the specialisation of small industrial countries towards industries with comparatively stable demands and low price elasticity (Maskell, 1998, p 194). In most cases this has included a strong reliance on resource processing industries, as reflected in the importance of metal, ore, paper, pulp and fish in the Nordic economies (Dalum and Villumsen, 1996). The Danish specialisation, for example, includes a long-standing bias towards meat, fish, dairy products, beer and related machine tool industries. Recently Denmark has gained ground in activities further removed from natural resource processing, but involving high value specialisations within traditional industries such as consumer goods (Lego), clothing, furniture and machinery. The nation's few high tech firms – in electronics, medical appliances and pharmaceuticals – often have origins in the agro-industrial sector. A further notable feature of Europe's small industrial countries is that the economic specialisations of the Nordic, Benelux and Austria-Switzerland groups tend to be distinctive from each other (Maskell, 1998). The extent of the squeeze also needs to be moderated by the fact that small countries by population are not necessarily small in land area or resources, as illustrated by Norway's high per capita wealth from its oil reserves.

Nonetheless the external vulnerability of small industrial countries is generally judged to have made their economic achievements particularly impressive (Katzenstein, 1985; Castles, 1988). Both large and small countries are vulnerable to the impact of technological and market changes, but in large economies, where there is a greater number of industries, it is more likely that these changes will 'average out'. A decline in employment in one part of the economy can be offset by growth in other parts of the economy. In the case of small open economies with specialised industrial structures, protection from the impacts of industrial change by an averaging out across growing and declining sectors is less likely than in a large economy (Landesmann and Varitiainen, 1992, p 213). The risks of social malaise and conflict, which might add to the challenge of managing economic change, are therefore greater in a small than a large economy. It emphasises a need to devise social agreements that maintain national cohesion. The specialisation of a small economy can be an advantage in achieving such accord where labour and employer organisations are centralised and where national economic management can be tailored to the needs of the dominant sector. Those opportunities were reflected in the corporatism of European small countries.

Small Country Corporatism and New Zealand Exceptionalism

A challenge to the small country category has been the difference in economic strategy and success as between New Zealand and Australia, on the one hand, and the European small nations on the other (Castles, 1988). This difference centres on the incorporation of interest groups into decision-making, welfare policy and trade openness. Broadly, while European small countries emphasise the sharing of political control with interest groups, strong welfare systems and open borders, New Zealand and Australia have had strong governments and weak interest groups, residual welfare systems and, at least until recently, trade protection. The suggestion that New Zealand's welfare system was 'residual' may seem strange given the popular impression of welfare profligacy. In fact New Zealand's social expenditure was not high in comparison with other small OECD countries. In 1981, for example, as a proportion of total public expenditure, New Zealand's social expenditure was below the OECD average and lessened only by Switzerland, Greece and (marginally) Australia (OECD, 1985). The welfare system was residual in that it concentrated on assistance to those permanently or temporarily out of work. Active labour market policies and subsidised job creation that characterised those economies with high welfare expenditure were not strongly funded in

New Zealand; instead trade protection became an alternative way of seeking to maintain full employment (Mabbett, 1995).

The corporatism of Europe's small industrial economies, as exemplified by Sweden, was organised around encompassing interest groups, and welfare systems designed to compensate those affected by economic change. This alignment facilitated the acceptance of market changes originating in international markets, a policy stance that was described as "rolling with the punches of economic fluctuations" made possible by the willingness to "live with change by compensating for it" (Katzenstein, 1985, p 24). Compensation for adjustment existed through active labour market policies which emphasised retraining and employment mobility. Other compensation comprised stabilisation and growth policies, such as Sweden's investment reserve to smooth fluctuations in the business cycle, and prices and incomes policies to prevent export commodities from being priced out of markets (Castles, 1988, p 87).

There are various interpretations of the origins of encompassing labour and employer organisations and how they came to accept compensation in return for trade openness. Katzenstein (1985) suggested that partnership and cooperation between peak organisations were responses to international vulnerability, which in the case of Europe's small industrial countries was heightened by the economic crisis of the 1930s and the Second World War which threatened the survival of some small states. Mabbett (1995, p 189) puts the emphasis on the way that both employers and labour in the internationally exposed sector came to see self-regulation as preferable to government intervention. Dominant labour unions were concerned to avoid centralised wage fixing and trade protection, as both were seen as potential threats to high income for export sector workers. Employer attitudes were a response to the extension of democracy. The extension of the franchise came later in Sweden (and other Nordic countries) than it did in New Zealand and only after campaigning by the formerly disenfranchised, including segments of the wage labouring classes. Employers in the competitive sector were not a numerically important group and they could not rely on there being a politically sympathetic government once the franchise was extended. The spectre of a pro-labour government and interventionist economic policies encouraged employers to be strategically organised and, initially, strongly opposed to trade union power. Aggressive employer action displaced weak craft unions but encouraged a strong central union that drew support from a Social

Democratic government indebted to the union role in the attainment of universal franchise. Encompassing unions in the export sector came to work with employers on the basis of a negotiated settlement which guaranteed the status of unions in return for assurance that centralised authority would be exerted over individual union members.

New Zealand followed the pattern of small industrial countries in having an open competitive sector in respect of primary produce, the key export industry. A protected manufacturing sector became an anomaly compared with the expectation of openness in a small economy. The ultimate explanation for this is linked to the modern economic origins in a settler society in which all sections of the community looked to the state for security and the development of necessary public services. As described further in chapter 4, state intervention took forms that dissipated the costs of the sheltered economy on the export sector. But intervention also slowed down transformation in the manufacturing economy. Trade protection became significant in post-war New Zealand because of the pessimistic appraisal of the potential for traditional exporters to diversify or expand exports and because the imperative of maintaining a population inflow demanded new sources of employment. The non-traditional exporters that emerged, predominantly large corporates, pressed for the 'rolling back of the state'. The success of this agenda extended trade openness across larger parts of the economy, creating conditions suitable for growth in the expanded competitive sector. This has brought New Zealand closer to the small industry country norm except that the reduction in the presence of the state has not seen any corresponding growth in self-regulation by strong interest groups. An alliance of corporate interests and an intellectually sympathetic state extended reform across labour market and welfare organisation and created furthering weakening and fragmentation of other interest groups.

Given the greater economic success of the European small economies as compared to New Zealand, it is tempting to endorse the corporatist arrangement of strong interest groups, compensatory welfare and trade openness as the preferred model. It certainly permitted the expansion and improvement of the manufacturing sector in ways that largely eluded New Zealand, but questions remain about the long-term success of the corporatist model. Compensation policies provided new employment mainly through public sector jobs that employed different labour groups (female) than those displaced from the competitive sector (male) without solving the need for employment expansion in the competitive private sector. Currency devaluation often played a more important role than flexible adjustment in sustaining competitiveness (Korkman, 1992), a policy that was less effective for New Zealand because of the low price elasticity for agricultural produce (Mabbett, 1995, p 120). Ultimately, expansion of the public sector became a burden on the export competitiveness sector just as trade protection did in New Zealand. As well, the divergence of interests between public and private sector workers gradually reduced the organisational cohesion of labour. The corporatist strategy has greater claims to being a sustainable model than resort to trade protection to the extent that the productivity loss from public sector growth was less than that from protection (Mabbett, 1995, p 131). In addition, compensation strategies supported the collective provision of household services and expansion in female work participation whereas trade protection preserved male employment domination and slowed down the pace of restructuring and social change.

Three main points emerge from the past contrast between Nordic corporatism and New Zealand trade protection:

• Nordic corporatism and New Zealand trade protection have been responses to essentially the same challenges facing all small industrial countries: how to maintain employment and income growth in vulnerable economies. Differences in public policy do not undermine the case for a small country phenomenon.

• The suggestion that small countries have an affinity with corporatism can be dismissed given that it never extended to all small countries and because there has been a weakening of corporatist arrangements where they formerly existed. On the other hand, a case may be made that interest group organisation has been a key influence on small country development. Encompassing, industry-based groups in the competitive sector are more compatible with the need to accommodate economic change than narrow, skill-based groups.

• Understanding the comparative origins of public policy arrangements identifies influences and differences that survive with implications for business behaviour (as explored further in chapter 3). In the Nordic economies, there is a history of self-regulation by strong interest groups. In New Zealand, interest groups have remained weak and small. Business support for employer groups can promote interaction within industries and it can encourage individual organisations to participate in collective strategies. As discussed below, it is claimed that such business cooperation has contributed to Nordic economic success.

Shared Trust

Recently it has been argued that being a small economy may offer an advantage in the relative ease of establishing trust between organisations (Maskell et al, 1998). Just as in a village compared with a city it may be difficult to act opportunistically without being firmly sanctioned, so in a small economy compared with a large the pressure to 'play by the rules' is said to increase (Maskell, 1998, p 198). Small economies should sustain shared trust more easily than medium-size and large economies because:

- The small number of players in the business community means that each participant has a high stake in their industry and an interest in its collective well-being.
- Cheating or opportunism is hard to hide amongst a small group. Transparency, plus the ability to sustain collective sanctions against mavericks, should reduce the likelihood of underhand or disruptive behaviour and lessen resistance to trustful cooperation.
- Personal familiarity across businesses should be high as a consequence of family ties; shared education and training institutions; and mutual participation in local, regional or national joint activity. In Denmark, for example, it is suggested that all firms are members of at least one sector group, with its own publications and meetings. Mutually understood beliefs, values and culture should facilitate the exchange of codified and tacit knowledge.
- While small economies may exist within large territories, the likelihood of geographical proximity amongst large parts of an industry is high facilitating face-to-face interaction. To the same degree, mobility between workplaces is less likely to remove persons from the network; rather, it becomes another strength to the system as contacts between businesses multiply.

The impact of shared trust may not be an unusual propensity to enter formal alliances, although where alliances form it is expected to make them particularly effective. Of first importance is that the risk of becoming a local outcast should reduce the incidence of unfair and disruptive competition. As well, there is expected to be a willingness to pool information and support projects of collective benefit (Maskell et al, 1998, p 94). None of this need be at the loss of business rivalry in the home market, because the openness of markets permits foreign competition and domestic industries may comprise many small competitors. The industrial specialisations of Nordic economies may have contributed to the influence of shared trust (Maskell et al, 1998). Medium and low technology industry increases the scope for stable relations between individual businesses and the promotion of collective learning. The same benefits would be hard to capture in industries affected by sudden shifts in technology and demand but they can be captured in the "quiet and less glorious road of low-tech learning" (Maskell, 1998, p 201). It may, therefore, be that activities in which inter-firm relations can be a source of competitive strength are the ones in which successful small economies have chosen to specialise.

Some support for the importance of shared trust has been claimed from statistical evidence showing the importance of supplier-buyer interaction in the creation of the competitive advantage of the small European states (Fagerberg, 1995). Direct evidence is claimed in a number of case studies of industries important to Nordic economies, including the Danish wooden furniture industry. In the 1990s, around 20% of all European Union furniture exports came from Denmark (Maskell et al, 1998, p 105). The industry is built upon small firms (average employment per firm has stayed below 40 since the 1970s) and is not distinguished from international competitors by its technology (most is now imported) or proprietary designs (up-market unique design accounts for only around 10% of the Danish industry). Rather, the industry's strength is attributed to subcontracting networks and associated investment cooperation that has encouraged a high level of automation and business specialisation. As well as coordinated investments in equipment, cooperation amongst trading partners is seen in the temporary exchange of personnel and loans of machinery, all possible without written contracts.

In Finland, the dominance of the forest sector by the pulp and paper industry has restricted the establishment of the wooden furniture industry as part of a general bias against small-firm industries. The Finnish economy is built around big organisations in the forest, chemical and now telecommunications sectors (Lilja and Tainio, 1996). Here, as in Sweden where big firms also dominate, shared trust is manifested through 'development pairs'. These might comprise a formal joint venture or simply a close working relationship between two organisations (Maskell et al, 1998, p 171). The extent of personal ties and common backgrounds among members of the paired organisations distinguishes such alliances from those found in large countries. This eases formation, raises the effectiveness of cooperation and combines expertise that would be less likely to come together in a large economy. Development pairs between public and private organisations have been a particular feature of the development of the Nordic telecommunications and power engineering industries, partly reflecting the participation of public agencies in these sectors as regulators, network operators and technology buyers. Differences in competence and work regimes that might otherwise frustrate effective cooperation between public and private sector bodies seem not to have been a problem helped, it is suggested, by the ability of individuals to move between sectors. The argument is as follows:

> The small country malfeasance-controlling environment is usually in itself sufficient to ensure an absence of the obvious problems inherent in such relocations (for example, bribes and other forms of corruption). (Maskell et al, 1998, p 171)

Questioning Shared Trust

It is interesting that Nordic researchers put a positive spin on the village-like qualities of a small economy. Shared trust may be reinforced by corporatist strategies and organised interest groups, but the suggestion that shared trust arises automatically in a small country is questionable. In New Zealand the negative possibilities of small communities might be thought as likely to arise as the positive (see the survey results in chapter 4 for some evidence of this). Within small communities, competition may be at the expense of neighbours and the potential for perceived unfairness is high, as with allegations of labour poaching. Collusion against third parties may also arise where a few established players are motivated to enforce solidarity against new entrants that threaten existing working practices and market shares. The openness of Nordic economies may have minimised these risks but there remain reasons to question the importance of shared trust.

Further evidence that demonstrates the power of Nordic shared trust is needed. Maskell et al (1998) present case studies of the wooden furniture and telecommunications industries to support their claims but these studies are open to alternative interpretations. Small-firm specialisation and subcontracting networks in the Danish wooden furniture industry may say less about the existence of shared trust than the economics of component assembly. As with other component industries, vertical disintegration exists because individual components have their own distinct technology and scale economy. Moreover, it is noted that the subcontracting ties within the industry were distinguished by their stability (Maskell et al, 1998, p 107), whereas one of the expected impacts of shared trust is the potential for extremely fluid relationships. As well, the success of the Danish industry is presumably connected to demand conditions in which interior design is generally regarded as an unusually high priority amongst Scandinavian consumers in general and Denmark especially. The contribution of a testing domestic market would seem to require investigation before concluding anything about shared trust. Whatever that shows, it is worth noting that the New Zealand furniture industry has not attained similar disintegration and this is a challenge to its long-term viability. In the Nordic telecommunications case, the role of development pairs (the claimed outcome of shared trust in this case) is hard to assess given that other advantages have also been important. For example, it is said that the "peculiarities of its demand conditions" have compensated for the small domestic market, particularly in requiring understanding of a diversity of user groups (Maskell et al, 1998, p 175). The linkage between private and public agencies in the development pairs reflects the context common in many countries where the respective roles of regulators, network operators and technology providers have been changing with the privatisation of telecommunications markets.

More broadly underpinning the claims about shared trust has been evidence of the importance of domestic buyer-supplier interaction in the economic specialisation of Nordic economies (Maskell et al, 1998, p 88). There is statistical analysis to substantiate this in the Nordic economies (Fagerberg, 1995). This evidence originates in the conditions for competitive success proposed by Porter (1990), whose diamond model has been viewed as inappropriate to New Zealand and other resource-based economies (Spring, 1992; Cartwright, 1993; Yetton et al, 1993). In particular, it has failed to recognise how New Zealand's most successful exporters often pursue a strategy of off-shore production and value adding, rendering domestic buyer-supplier interaction unimportant.

For the present, reservations about the operation of shared trust make the concept of interest for two reasons:

(i)   it draws attention to a potentially important aspect of being a small country that has generally been given little attention; and
(ii)   for small countries without shared trust, it identifies a possible way of strengthening business performance.

Small Countries in a Borderless World

The influence of the small country category may be questioned from the perspective that increasing international economic integration is reducing the relevance of the nation state. These forces include the growth of new, non-national economic actors including truly global corporations, the expansion of international capital markets and the growth of international trade (Chase-Dunn, 1989; Dicken, 1998). The resulting capacity to coordinate economic activities across international borders can reduce the dependency that individual organisations have to individual national territories. Within Europe, such claims have been given added force by the expansion of the European Union, and moves to a single European market and currency. In this context the 'reach' of national regulation is undoubtedly challenged but the extent of actual change needs to be kept in proportion.

As shown above, small countries remain unusual in their high degree of trade openness (Table 2.1). Neither has the growth of foreign direct investment yet been able to produce the dominance of placeless global corporations. For most multinational firms, the home country and home region provide distinguishing attributes and allegiances. Leading multinational corporations from the Netherlands, for example, sell around 12% of their turnover to domestic customers but another 50% goes to customers in neighbouring European countries (Whitley, 1999, p 121). Moreover, with a few exceptions including New Zealand, inward foreign direct investment is a small share of total output in a small industrial economy (Table 2.5). The growth of international financial markets has similarly yet to eclipse the primary reliance on domestic and regional financial markets (Hirst and Thompson, 1996).

As well as the need to keep the scale of globalising trends in proportion, the process through which national entities might be converted into qualitatively different types of organisation limits the speed of change

(Whitley, 1999). For example, while inward foreign direct investment has the potential to break down national systems of management, such an impact will depend on:

(i)   the scale of inward investment relative to the size of the host economy, with high impact likely to depend on incoming business being focused on one or a few sectors that occupy a central position in the host economy;

(ii)   foreign firms sharing management methods that differ strongly from those in the host economy;

(iii) the independence of introduced methods from host country institutions and regulations, that otherwise would require adjustment amongst incoming businesses; and

(iv)   inward investment retaining strong linkages to its home country that reduce the need to adapt to host economy characteristics.

With respect to the transformation of business practice in New Zealand as a consequence of inward investment, this has already occurred. The legacy of the British dependency, perpetuated by reliance on foreign capital and immigration, has resulted in many of the key domestic institutions being 'Anglo Saxon'. The other main source of influence on the economy is Australia, another Anglo Saxon economy (Marceau, 1992). Contemporary investment flows from alternative business cultures are not on a scale to challenge this heritage.

The likelihood of internationalisation reducing national distinctiveness exists in the case of the Nordic small economies and other European cases which have deviated from the Anglo Saxon model. The greater integration of these small economies in the international economy is making it harder to sustain corporatist structures. Externally, the regional integration of capital markets reduces the scope for independent interest and exchange rate policies, an important development since currency devaluation has been an important aspect of economic management amongst the Nordic states (Korkman, 1992). The growth of inward and outward flows of foreign direct investment reduces the potential responsiveness of business to measures aimed at strengthening the domestic market. Internally, greater fragmentation of labour markets and business types is decreasing the influence of centralised bargaining and reducing the influence of labour and employer groups. On the other hand, it should be noted that

Table 2.5 National Variations in Inward and Outward Foreign Direct Investment 1980 and 1996

	Inward stock as % of GDP		Outward stock as % of GDP	
	1980	1996	1980	1996
Large countries:				
– USA[1]	3.1	8.3	8.1	10.4
– Japan	0.3	0.7	1.9	5.6
Medium-sized countries:				
– France	3.4	10.1	3.6	13.1
– Germany	4.5	5.9	5.3	12.4
– Italy	2.0	7.4	1.6	10.6
– Spain	2.4	18.1	0.6	6.7
– UK	11.7	20.5	14.9	30.7
Nordic countries:				
– Denmark	6.3	13.4	3.1	12.9
– Finland	1.1	7.1	1.4	14.3
– Iceland	—	2.7	1.8	3.3
– Norway	11.4	13.0	3.2	18.0
– Sweden	2.9	13.7	4.5	28.3
Non-Nordic small countries:				
– Australia	8.7	29.7	1.5	11.7
– Austria	4.1	8.5	0.7	5.8
– Belgium & Luxembourg	6.0	45.8	4.9	31.4
– Canada	20.4	22.0	9.0	21.3
– Greece	11.3	16.6	—	0.7
– Netherlands	11.3	30.4	24.9	49.1
– New Zealand	10.5	51.8	5.8	14.6
– Portugal	4.4	6.4	0.5	3.3

Notes:
1.   1995.

Source: World Investment Report, 1998.

integration with the European Union provides some countervailing influences with respect to trade union rights and 'social contracts'.

Corporatist small states are likely to adapt rather than disappear entirely. Nordic social scientists now tend to discuss their distinctiveness in terms of being a 'negotiated economy' rather than a corporate state (Nielsen and Pedersen, 1991; Amin and Thomas, 1996). Even in the case of Denmark where encompassing interest groups have been less important than in other small European states, contemporary descriptions of political management continue to suggest a legacy of organised interest groups that provide a distinctive business environment.

> Small nations such as Denmark have a tradition for working out broad compromises between stakeholders in business, politics and public life *in toto*. The consensus-seeking behaviour is rooted in a special sort of collective learning that takes place when all participants know that their chance of success in international business critically depends on the strength of domestic unity. Dissatisfied partners or neighbours result in continuous problems, which will have negative effects on all. The collective learning ... seems to convey the message that yielding on some point in order to reach a compromise will often give better long-term results, than does taking full advantage of a contemporary strong bargaining position ...

> Few who have witnessed the functioning of the negotiated economy at close quarters are likely to feel tempted to praise its simplicity or effectiveness. However, its merit lies on another level: in the way in which the process of reaching an agreement or decision simultaneously increases the insight in – and understanding of – the other participant's positions, interests and visions. (Maskell, 1998, pp 196-197)

Conclusion

A distinctive small country experience originates in four shared characteristics. First, there is an exceptional dependency on overseas markets and exposure to international competition. These attributes encourage small economies to specialise on a comparatively narrow range of activities.

Exposure and specialisation result in vulnerability to market changes. Second, small industrial economies have limited capacity to participate in high technology sectors and typically specialise in low to medium technology exports. Third, the extent and form of interest group organisation has differentiated small industrial economies with consequences for the adaptability to economic change. Encompassing, industry-based groups have facilitated restructuring to a greater extent than narrow and weak interest groups. The extension of this argument to the claim that small industrial countries have a 'natural' affinity with corporatism is not sustainable, but smallness and economic vulnerability may help maintain encompassing groups where they have arisen. Four, in a small economy individual business managers are more likely to be personally known to each other, to share the same values and to have a higher stake in their industry than in a large business community. Nordic research suggests that this encourages shared trust and cooperation amongst business managers in ways that stimulate innovation and industry competitiveness. That claim needs further evidence but it does draw attention to the general proposition that the strength of small business communities is highly susceptible to the quality of relations between business managers.

Europe's small economies seem to have captured the advantages arising in a small state to a greater extent than New Zealand. The greater challenge facing a small economy with an agricultural specialisation is one possible explanation for the performance difference. An open border for New Zealand's main tradeable sector has had comparatively little impact in either improved market access or overall production efficiency. This constraint does not provide all the explanations for New Zealand's weakness. Resource-based industries have been important in successful small economies and they have also had to find ways of managing vulnerability arising from dependence on foreign income. As well, it would be wrong to see New Zealand's agricultural reliance as an immutable structural feature of the economy. There has been a long and largely unsuccessful effort to shed this agricultural dependence. That failure is suggestive of deep-seated weaknesses in private sector entrepreneurship. In this regard, examining New Zealand against the performance of other small industrial economies may be seen as instructive in terms of their broadly similar constraints and opportunities. One contrast has existed in the style of economic management. The corporatism of the Nordic states proved unsustainable and in the long run has weakened for similar reasons to New Zealand's retreat from its former economic management (Mabbett, 1995). A legacy of encompassing interest groups may have been an influence on the presence of shared trust.

There has been little attention paid to the level of trust within New Zealand's business community. Even without decisive evidence to demonstrate its contribution to Nordic economic success, there are reasons to investigate the environment for business cooperation in New Zealand. Sustaining trust in a small community may be harder than the Nordic proponents of shared trust envisage but it may be viewed as a desired condition, in which case investigation is warranted to determine the influences that sustain shared trust and its current status. Such an investigation is conducted over the next chapters commencing in chapter 3 with an explanation of why business behaviour in New Zealand may be expected to be less cooperative than that in Nordic countries. This discussion takes us back to the origins of corporatist arrangements in Europe, the reasons for New Zealand's different institutional history and the legacies these contrasting political settlements have had on business organisation.

Endnotes

1. The use of 'industrial' may seem inappropriate given New Zealand's dependence on primary sector exports. Industrial in this context implies developed, high income economies to differentiate these small economies from the newly industrialising and low income small economies. The population threshold of 25 million poses a problem in classifying Canada as its population exceeded this threshold in the 1980s. It has been retained within the small country category in the data presented in this study.

2. The data presented for small industrial countries are based on the sample of small countries included in the OECD STAN database. These data include all Nordic countries, Australia and New Zealand but omit several European small countries.

3. The OECD report does not include a comparable New Zealand figure.

3 • Business Systems and Small Country Differences

The previous chapter has argued that the common characteristics of small industrial economies present them with distinctive challenges compared with larger economies. Others have argued that the only thing small countries have in common is that each is different (Amstrup, 1976). Historical experiences, political systems and approaches to economic management have created differences amongst small industrial economies. This is evident in the Nordic proclivity for corporatist economic management compared with the Anglo Saxon systems preferred in New Zealand. As well, small economies have enjoyed differences in economic success. 'Shared trust' may provide one explanation for the industrial strength observed in the Nordic economies because of the way it can make cooperation between independent businesses easier to establish than in a medium or large-sized country. Benefits are claimed to arise in terms of increased information sharing, specialisation and innovation.

Shared trust is seen to originate in two attributes of a small economy: first, the high level of personal familiarity and shared values amongst owners and managers; two, curbs on malfeasance in a close-knit business community. As suggested by the contrasting economic performance of small economies, these attributes are not inevitable in a small economy. Personal ties may, for example, be less significant in a geographically expansive state than in a confined territory, although with modern communications any such barriers ought to be reducing.

This chapter examines the barriers to shared trust arising in the characteristics of small country 'business systems'. Business systems theory is an area of academic enquiry that seeks to explain differences in business organisation and to identify the interconnections between the organisational options that exist within market economies. It examines the impact of political and economic management on business behaviour and argues that places are associated with distinctive patterns of business behaviour.

This chapter introduces business system perspectives that can help in assessing the significance of shared trust in smaller industrial economies. Subsequent chapters will look at the status of shared trust in New Zealand and the scope for public policy to promote business cooperation.

Business Systems

Around the capitalist industrial world, amongst similar and different-sized economies, the organisation of markets and industries varies. Business systems theory provides a framework for analysing and explaining these differences. These ideas originate in the work of Richard Whitley (1992, 1999) who has been impressed by the contrasts in business behaviour within East Asia's new industrial economies as well as between business organisations in these economies and that in western countries. Recognition of these contrasts indicates that economic success is associated with many different ways of organising business. Hence, for Whitley and other business system adherents, divergence in business practice is the outstanding characteristic of economic globalisation rather than convergence to a uniform way of conducting business. Distinctive patterns of economic organisation are expected to survive because of the diverse influences that shape business behaviour. Many of these influences have their origins in historical processes whose influence erodes slowly, if at all, as well as from contemporary institutions and competitive opportunities. Whitley's ideas are utilised in this chapter to justify the claim that contrasting institutional histories have made New Zealand's business system less cooperative than those existing in Nordic economies.

In his most recent account of business system processes, Whitley (1999) identifies three main ways that market economies may differ.

1. *Ownership coordination*: Management of business organisations is frequently separated from ownership within industrial economies. The management-ownership separation varies, explained partly by differences in the importance of small-scale enterprise. Direct control by owner managers is more characteristic of small rather than big business. The predominant form of business finance also shapes management-ownership relations. Credit-based financial systems are more frequently associated with direct, long-term relations between the lender and borrower than are capital-based systems. In institutional terms, this is a distinction based on the relative

importance of bank (credit) and equity market (capital) sources of business finance. The significance of the difference is greatest where the capital suppliers take a small share of ownership and are primarily concerned to maintain a diversified portfolio of liquid investments. Credit suppliers, on the other hand, can favour a long-term relationship as the context for supplying a range of services to client businesses and their employees. Credit-based systems are thus associated with the development of 'alliance ownership' in which the owners (typically banks) retain commitment to the individual organisations owned. This commitment can produce insight into the technologies, products and markets of the firms in which they have substantial investments. Where the bank concentrates assets in one or a few sectors, this enables them to transfer their management insight across business boundaries and to reduce their exposure to risk by coordinating investment in their sectors of influence. In contrast, capital providers tend to rely on broad financial indicators to monitor the performance of their assets and this brings less insight than alliance owners can obtain through an ongoing relationship. A further implication is that capital markets tend to encourage precise ownership boundaries around individual businesses. Overlapping ownership boundaries and diffuse linkages can make it hard for portfolio managers to gather data on individual enterprises and to liquidate investments.

2. *Non-ownership coordination*: Alliances, obligations and other preferential relations integrate business without the need for ownership ties. Three main opportunities arise:

    (i)   independent buyers and suppliers can sustain a high degree of production chain integration through reciprocal trading relations;
    (ii) collaboration with competitors; and
    (iii) cross-sector coordination.

    Across these three opportunities, business system analysis stresses the contrast between business relations dominated by adversarial relations focused on short-term advantage and those which stress mutual benefits and long-term development opportunities.

3. *Employment and work management*: Business systems vary in the

dominant way that employers reconcile the need for workforce productivity with the capacity to adjust employment according to market needs. In some cases, the emphasis is on minimum impediments to redundancy and external recruitment; in other cases, the emphasis is on functional flexibility and mutual commitment within the context of a long-term employment obligation. The use of external labour markets is affected by the influence attained by independent trade unions, and whether they are organised around labour skills, individual workplaces or industries. Enterprise or industry-based unions are generally more propitious for employer-employee cooperation as well as broader intra-sectoral collaboration than skill-based unions. On the other hand, skill and industry-based unions are both potentially consistent with centralised bargaining between employers and employees coordinated by employers' groups and union federations. Centralised bargaining, in turn, can facilitate other forms of collaboration where it brings individual employers together on a continuing basis.

The manner through which labour skills are developed and controlled plus the broader organisation of labour markets are further sources of business system diversity. The extent to which employers, trade unions and public agencies jointly participate in the certification of labour skills varies and influences the extent to which the training system promotes generic or firm-specific skills. Another differentiating attribute is the relative status of general and vocational education. In a dual education system, vocational training is serviced by high status institutions that offer an alternative to an academic learning track. In unitary education systems, participation in vocational training is mainly by being performance-judged out of the academic system into a secondary stream. The dual-track system combines practical skills with academic education. Workforce qualifications so produced may exceed immediate workplace needs. The benefit to business can be an enlarged capacity for future learning, and adaptability to changes in technology and work organisation.

Links Between Business System Components

The individual business system components are interlinked and usually it requires the existence of mutually reinforcing attributes to obtain a significant impact on business behaviour from individual components. These combinations set limits to the range of business systems that can exist. Whitley (1999) identifies six combinations that equate with the main types of business system that can be identified around the industrial world (see Table 3.1). None of these ideal types matches either New Zealand or the Nordic countries, although the compartmentalised and collaborative business systems respectively share some features in common with the countries of interest to this study as well as some notable differences. Before discussing in more detail the differences between New Zealand and Nordic business systems, a brief outline of these ideal types is useful as they provide a benchmark for comparison.

Compartmentalised business systems, which are best illustrated by the Anglo Saxon capitalism practised in North America and Great Britain, arise where large business units and market control dominate. Market control means that owners exercise influence at arm's length through financial markets with priority to portfolio diversification and investment liquidity rather than sector specialisation and a long-term ownership commitment. The comparatively short-term commitment of owners is a constraint on the development of inter-firm collaboration. As a consequence, significant risk-sharing within production chains or amongst competitors is unlikely to develop, especially as market owners prefer clear organisational boundaries. Diffuse networks around ownership units can be perceived as a problem when valuing assets and comparing returns in the absence of the detailed insight that can be acquired by alliance owners. On the other hand, diversification into unrelated activities is encouraged to manage ownership risks and this growth path can result in multi-activity conglomerates. For the same reasons that the impetus to long-term cooperation between businesses is reduced, market control is a constraint on high levels of employer-employee interdependence. Employers are comparatively free to utilise external labour markets to adjust employment in line with changes in market conditions and this flexibility is generally favoured over long-term employment commitments.

Collaborative business systems, which Whitley suggests are best illustrated by European economies with strong corporatist structures, are distinguished by their propensity for collective organisation and cooperation within sectors. These business systems include alliance forms of ownership that, as previously noted, encourage business commitment to their industry. Owners that are locked into the fates of particular firms

Table 3.1 Whitley's Six Types of Business System

Business system attributes	Business system type					
	Fragmented	Coordinated	Compart-mentalised	State organised	Collaborative	Highly coordinated
Ownership coordination:						
– owner control	Direct	Direct	Market	Direct	Alliance	Alliance
– ownership integration of production chains	Low	Low	High	High	High	Some
– ownership integration of sectors	Low	Low	High	Some to high	Limited	Limited
Non-Ownership coordination:						
– alliance coordination of production chains	Low	Limited	Low	Low	Limited	High
– collaboration between competitors	Low	Some	Low	Low	High	High
– alliance coordination of sectors	Low	Low	Low	Low	Low	Some
Employment relations:						
– employer-employee interdependence	Low	Some	Low	Low	Some	High
– delegation to employees	Low	Some	Low	Low	High	Considerable

Source: Whitley (1999).

have an incentive to form risk-sharing relations with other enterprises, both within production chains and amongst competitors. This integration is reinforced by the demonstration of industry commitment as one of the tests of a reliable business partner. Industry lock-in is also an influence on employer-employee interdependence. Employers are open to cooperation with industry training bodies, possibly including trade union participation, to support the development of industry and firm-specific skills. For employees, this can mean a loss of generic skills and less emphasis on externally accredited professional expertise which, in turn, means a loss of employment mobility. To offset this, employers are obliged to minimise 'hire and fire' approaches and to accept a responsibility to retain skilled employees through periods of recession. This can raise the expectations of employees with respect to their status in the workplace, whilst also responding to employer needs for an industry-skilled workforce that can be entrusted with significant task delegation.

As noted above, although some conforming attributes can be found, it is over-simplistic to describe the Nordic economies as collaborative and New Zealand as compartmentalised. In the case of New Zealand, as later sections discuss, the compartmentalised business system has been shaped primarily by the influence of the state over economic relations, rather than the dominance of large organisations, which has raised distinctive issues. In the case of the Nordic economies, there are differences in the economic structures and political systems of individual countries that need to be acknowledged (Kristensen et al, 1996; Schienstock et al, 1998). Across the Nordic diversity, it is not so much specific forms of business organisation that are shared so much as the unusual degree of national cohesion. There was in the past an emphasis on credit rather than capital markets which produced a more strategic allocation of finance to industry than would have happened had the Nordic countries relied largely on equity markets (Landesmann and Vartiainen, 1992, p 225). This strategy was frequently expressed through efforts to mediate collaboration within groups of enterprises belonging to the bank's sectoral specialisations (Kristensen, 1996). This strategy was most influential in the case of those Nordic countries dominated by large industrial groups (Finland and Sweden). In Denmark, the dominance of credit-based finance including regional savings banks and building societies supported the survival of independent enterprise rather than alliance ownership (Kristensen, 1996). Across the Nordic region the distinctiveness of its financial system has reduced through deregulation and the consolidation of bank ownership.

Communal Authority and Nordic Business Systems

The basis on which business transactions are conducted is given a great amount of attention in the explanation of the origins of individual business systems. All transactions rely on a degree of trust between the trading parties. There are two main ways that trust is sustained. One way is through the mutual confidence in institutions and legal procedures that can be utilised in the event of disputes. There are some business systems that have not attained this confidence, as with Chinese family enterprise in Southeast Asia which instead relies on personal and kinship connections as the basis for establishing exchange relationships. A second type of trust originates in a strong conception of national interest that encourages shared understandings of priorities and interests, producing what Whitley recognises as a communal form of authority.

Communal forms of authority imply higher levels of mutual trust and commitment than where trust is based on formal sources of authority alone. Contractual sources of trust are stronger in controlling malicious behaviour than they are in encouraging proactive cooperation. The presence of communal authority is expected to have two main consequences for business organisation and behaviour, both of which are conducive to inter-firm cooperation (Whitley, 1999):

1. The freedom of businesses to diversify into unrelated activities is reduced. Where communitarian conceptions of authority remain strong, workforce expectations constrain managers to demonstrate commitment to their existing skill base. Shifts in the core expertise of the business are likely to devalue existing work skills and are thus constrained by the expected commitment to existing activities. This limits change but helps sustain the perception of common identities and loyalties which employers can utilise to enable considerable task delegation to staff. In return for this delegation, employers seek to capture greater employee contribution to improvement than in environments where work responsibilities are tightly controlled by management. As well, employers trade reduced access to the external labour market against greater employer-employee interdependence. Compensation is, therefore, expected in the ability to delegate work responsibilities and to accommodate technology and market changes.

2. Intermediary associations representing industry and workforce interests are more likely to be effective where communal authority exists than where society lacks such cohesion. Where there are agreed goals and common interests individuals are more willing to delegate authority to collective organisations than where values and priorities are divided. In turn, the state is more likely to tolerate strong intermediary associations where these associations have a clear mandate from their members aligned to the national development goals. The influence of intermediary associations is also linked to the heightened industry commitment of businesses that, as noted above, is expected with communal authority. Where the fate of a business is locked into a particular sector, risk sharing with other industry participants is likely to be encouraged, for example, to regulate new entrants and coordinate investment in new technology. Similarly trade union participation in industry training and skill certification systems is less threatening to businesses that are tied into an industry specialisation than it generally is to businesses without such commitment.

In his account of small European states, Katzenstein (1985, p 32) argued that the "politics of domestic compensation" had sustained communal authority. This political style shared three defining traits: first, a national "ideology of social partnership" designed to reduce conflicts within society and minimise impediments to policy development; second, a comprehensive system of interest group organisations encompassing "a very large proportion of producers and workers" and operating through centralised 'peak' associations that make the number of principal actors small enough for effective negotiations; and, third, "voluntary and informal coordination of conflicting objectives involving continuous political bargaining among interest groups, bureaucracies and political parties". Katzenstein traced this political style to the 1930s and 1940s when the survival of many of Europe's small industrial countries was in doubt. The perceived threat came, in varying proportions, from depression, the rise of extreme political movements and external invasion. These threats:

> … broadened narrow conceptions of class interest to include
> acute awareness of the fragility of the small European states
> in a hostile world. An increasingly liberal international

economy in the postwar years offered daily confirmation of that awareness. International competition intensified, underlining the enormous benefits of limiting domestic conflicts over economic issues. (Katzenstein, 1985, p 36)

The timing of the search for a national compromise was significant as the Nordic economies were late industrialisers and before the Second World War still had large peasant populations. A defensive response, preserving things as they were, would have meant the acceptance of poverty and exploitation (Castles, 1989, p 43).

Katzenstein's interpretation of the role of Nordic welfare policies has been questioned as they tended to have more impact on promoting social change, especially in terms of female employment, rather than in compensating the actual victims of economic change (Mabbett, 1995). In this way welfare intervention was more successful in retaining solidarity between labour groups than it was at promoting economic adjustment. During the 1990s, the general pattern has been that welfare intervention has been cut back in the interests of export competitiveness and in response to increased divisions between private and public sector workers. As well, Mabbett (1995, p 189) questions whether it was external threat or concern about the possible consequences of government intervention that drove employer and labour interests to seek accommodation with each other. Whatever the precise mechanisms and origins, there is no doubt that Nordic political systems have retained the active engagement of interest groups in the negotiation of societal goals. Proportional representation voting systems have been an important part of this because they have encouraged governments to form broad-based alliances beyond the sectional interests of individual parties.

The connection between 'low voltage' politics, interest group representation and business cooperation has been made by Nordic social scientists in their discussions of the negotiated economy, an idea that was introduced in the previous chapter. The concept of the negotiated economy was developed originally to acknowledge how the organisation of business activity in Norway was shaped by the inter-play of private, semi-private and public institutions (Berrefjord and Heum, 1993; Christiansen, 1994). It has subsequently been applied to Denmark where it has been used to demonstrate how a high degree of economic coordination has been achieved despite the absence of a strong state and the fragmentation of business including a large population of small craft-based industries (Nielsen and Pedersen, 1988; Pedersen et al, 1992; Amin and Thomas, 1996; Maskell, 1998). Coordination is achieved by the activities of diverse consensus-seeking bodies, typically comprising representatives of the largest firms, employer federations, industry associations, trade unions, higher education and similar institutions. These bodies have been used to steer change through negotiation and are dependent on the active participation of business owners, professionals and unions in their interest associations. Maskell (1998), for example, discusses the role of an industrial development council in promoting strategy studies for each of the Denmark's main export clusters. Perersen et al (1992) discuss the involvement of various interest groups in gaining a consensus over the restructuring of certain food processing cooperatives into two major public corporations, a restructuring initially resisted by the farmer-owned cooperatives. Consensual decision-making in negotiated economies is based on the perception that in a small industrial economy the community at large are stakeholders in key development issues. This perception justifies investment in policy communities before taking major decisions. For its critics, this can be seen as a slow and cumbersome way of acting, while, for its supporters, it is seen as a way of making decisions in ways that retain national cohesion (Amin and Thomas, 1996).

New Zealand and the Politics of Domestic Defence
It has been argued that the politics of domestic defence were the Australia-New Zealand equivalent of the Nordic politics of domestic compensation (Castles, 1985, 1988, 1989). Whereas the Nordic approach is characterised as one of rolling with the punches of economic fluctuation, Australia and New Zealand pursued a defensive strategy that was designed to block the impact of economic change (Castles, 1988, p 93).

This comparison was developed primarily from Australian experience and fits less comfortably with New Zealand's economic and social policies, although the outcome in terms of limited industrial transformation was similar. The interpretation developed by Castles has recently been augmented and reinterpreted in a comparative investigation of New Zealand and Sweden (Mabbett, 1995). These accounts, based on the comparative history of trade, employment and welfare policies, provide the main sources for the following section. It first outlines the characteristics of key participants in New Zealand's business system and the influence they had on the institutions that have shaped business behaviour.

The State

In New Zealand, the state has operated with less need to negotiate and compromise with interest groups than is the pattern in a corporatist economy where an obligation to share power with union and employer organisations is central to their politics. The strength of the state has been reflected in its propensity to intervene in economic management and business development rather than to encourage self-management by and amongst interest groups. The comparative independence of the state from sectional interests arose from several influences.

1. Universal suffrage came early to New Zealand and prior to the organisation of labour unionisation or competitive employers. No political party was indebted to any sectional interest for its ability to participate in national politics as it was where the extension of the franchise was fought for by organised labour or strongly resisted by elites threatened by a loss of influence. This depressed the need for organisation amongst interest groups as individuals had relatively easy access to government whatever the political party in power.
2. The willingness to accept an extension of the state's role was influenced by the context of a new settler society. Located far away from the European centre of capital and population, an active state could credibly claim to be following the national interest given needs to acquire foreign loans, build infrastructure and control immigration in the interests of existing settlers.
3. The first-past-the-post electoral system encouraged political parties to appeal to national rather than sectional interests. In a proportional system, no party is likely to gain a majority, and to this extent remaining aligned to one interest group is less of a handicap. The consequence in New Zealand is that neither Labour nor National has been held in a straitjacket by their alignment to labour and farmers, and both parties have had the freedom to establish their own agenda.
4. Farmers had both political and economic power and were advocates of state involvement in economic development. This contrasts with situations where economic elites perceived a threat in the extension

of the state where it was associated with increased democratisation. The political power of farmers was strengthened by the use of the 'country quota'. That operated until 1945 and added 28% to the population of rural districts when allocating representation.

Trade Unions

The distinctive aspects of trade unions have been their craft-based organisation and overall weakness. Craft-based unionism is less supportive of industrial change than sector-based unionism because, for the individual union, restructuring of employment and changes in job definitions and demarcations posed the threat of membership loss. Union membership was high because of legislation (unions had monopoly rights of participation in the negotiation of wages and work conditions and for a time compulsory membership was enforced), but active participation by members was low as was the overall organisational capacity of unions. National awards governed conditions and so there was little active union involvement in the workplace. Industrial unionism was of some influence in the export sector amongst casual workers without craft skills. It remained a form of unionism that was opposed by the dominant craft unions whose status depended on the legislative system in which they participated. Craft unions protected their members from competition for employment that encouraged surplus labour to concentrate in the export sector. This division was reflected in the formation of rival pan-union organisations, the Federation of Labour for craft unions and the short-lived Trade Union Congress for more militant unions (a division which resurfaced in the early 1990s with a split between the Council of Trade Unions and the Trade Union Federation).

Employers

From an early stage, New Zealand had a comparatively modern employment structure in that manufacturing and agriculture were both important sources of employment. Manufacturing was predominantly for the domestic market while the rural sector supplied export markets. Both sectors remained the domain of small proprietorship who looked to government for support. Manufacturers sought protection from competition of which the main threat, given the country's 'natural' protection from imports, came from new entrants grabbing market share by undercutting wages and deviating from 'standard' labour practices. The rural economy sought the development of supporting infrastructure and control of the export chain. Farmer cooperatives and licensing of processing factories partly attended to the control sought by the rural sector. Union militancy in the processing factories and on the waterfront remained a threat. That risk was reduced by the preponderance of casual and unskilled labour employed in export chain activities. They existed outside the dominant craft-based union system. This provided an accommodation between rural and manufacturing sectors. Protection of manufacturing imposed a cost to the rural sector (through the high price of manufactured goods) but also a bulwark against industrial unionism and mechanisms that enabled firms to draw on the state to quell industrial unrest.

Industrial Relations

The legalistic control of industrial relations through the industrial conciliation and arbitration (IC&A) system, originally introduced in 1894 and substantially intact up to 1987 (Deeks et al, 1994), was central to the business system. It gave to government the authority to set national wage awards and working conditions for registered occupations. Registration under the IC&A system was dependent on union representation of the labour group receiving an award, giving government influence over the form of labour organisation. In corporatist economies, such power to intervene in industrial relations was denied the state because the dominant factions of labour and business preferred self-regulation. For New Zealand's manufacturers, the IC&A system gave incumbents protection against 'sweaters' and other new entrants by enforcing industry compliance to established wage norms and labour practices. It also set legal boundaries to the activities of registered unions that curtailed the scope for industrial action (unions were prevented from many actions that might have encouraged militancy such as the ability to accumulate strike funds or offer financial support to other unions on strike) and made the state a party in serious industrial disputes, because strikes were usually unlawful. The reality of small workplaces, in which a certain informality of work practices exists, made the controls less onerous than for larger employers. For unions, it provided protection against unilateral employer action and gave legal status to the skills they represented and the work demarcations on which they depended.

The IC&A system could be seen to suit the sheltered manufacturing sector but not the export economy where incomes varied widely according to the vagaries of commodity markets. Retention of the system could be explained partly by the absence of unions from the farm workforce. As well, craft unionism in the manufacturing sector in some ways assisted exporters. It resulted in surplus labour for less regulated occupations than those covered by skill-based unions. This work was often in export processing activities such as in the freezing works and on the waterfront where much employment became casual or seasonal. Exporters gained another benefit in that they could draw on the enforcement authority of the state to control serious outbreaks of industrial unrest.

The IC&A system reduced the need for groups to organise and engage with each other and this acted against the formation of strong employer or union groups. Incumbent employers obtained some protection against employers undercutting wages and expansion-minded entrepreneurs seeking enhanced efficiency. Attempts to use less-skilled labour than the norm, for example, could be stymied by the application of award provisions to employment levels and work organisation. Other divisions arose because of the varying conditions of regional labour markets that produced tension between employers as to the appropriate wage level and adjustments. Disputes technically between unions and employers were in some cases actually arguments amongst employers from different parts of the country (Holt, 1986, p 45). The generally weak representation of unions preserved managerial prerogatives but in the context of the control of competition that reduced the impetus to pursue productivity growth and challenge union-protected skill demarcations. Additions to award wages were largely at the prerogative of employers. Unions had limited organisational capacity to take the initiative in workplace negotiations, so that above-award payments might be seen by rival employers as attempts to poach labour. In the context of skilled labour shortages and the perceived expense of training, this was potentially a major source of friction between small employers.

The system's other important impact was to reduce employee commitment to the workplace. Protection of craft skills facilitated operation of the external labour market by providing externally accredited skills. Task demarcations reduced the likelihood of workplace-specific competences developing. Employers tended to invest little in training and instead relied on the apprenticeship system and independent training establishments. National awards separated the wage fortunes of workers from the economic health of enterprises and from other groups of workers.

In this system, the shortage of alternative opportunities outside the main cities and the close working ties that might arise in a small workplace were perhaps the main sources of loyalty for many employees. Otherwise there was no obvious basis on which trust between workers and employers could be built as was evident when the issue of workplace reform gained prominence in the late 1980s (Perry et al, 1995).

Tariff and Import Licensing
The slowing down of industrial change encouraged by the IC&A system was reinforced by trade protection that became important in the post-war years. There were connections between the two areas of policy in that wage control enabled trade protection to deliver social welfare objectives (for those in employment, wages and working conditions were defended) without public sector expansion. Trade protection is a potential burden on the export sector which the IC&A system helped to contain through the state's ability to influence wage levels. This approach to welfare provision fitted the preference of economic interest groups for employment stability and tightly drawn transfers contingent upon economic location. The comparison is with encompassing organisations in a corporatist system that are more likely to support broader forms of compensation including, for example, transfers that fund active labour market policies contingent on the acceptance of employment change.

The greater resort to import controls and tariff protection responded to pessimism over the potential to expand traditional exports or diversify into new markets. The resulting strategy of import substitution had several outcomes for business organisation:

1. The allocation of import licensing tended to be guided by economies of scale rather than the promotion of competition. Given the small size of the domestic market, a monopolistic industrial structure tended to result. Foreign suppliers of components and materials had an incentive to take part-ownership of firms which had a licensing history so as to receive preferential treatment in the allocation of licences (Hawke, 1985, p 274). Linkage between foreign suppliers and importers thus became more important than linkage between New Zealand enterprises.
2. The goal of diversified economic development acted against national specialisation, and especially against specialisation built upon

industries with highly developed interfirm collaboration. Rather truncated value chains tended to be encouraged. In the car assembly industry, for example, knocked down kits imported from the home country of the foreign owner were reassembled with few linkages to local component suppliers.

3.   A new target for business lobbying was created in the obtaining and retaining of trade protection. This displaced interest in innovation and technical change to the extent that these activities became an alternative and more burdensome basis for business success. This was reflected in the "spectacular growth" of the Manufacturers' Federation after import controls were introduced in 1938 (Rudman cited in Vowles, 1992, p 359).

Finance Markets and Corporate Ownership

The major private financial institutions in New Zealand evolved from their British counterparts during the relatively early days of European settlement (Skully, 1985). Consequently, the banking system followed the methods developed in Britain with their emphasis on short-term loans, secured in such a way that if the need arose the bank would have no difficulty in realising its security and liquidating the loan (Hawke, 1997, p 44). Although the predominantly foreign-owned banks were not necessarily resource-rich in New Zealand, they did not become tied to industrial groups as happened in the Nordic countries. Later legislation (the 1956 Trustee Act) limited the range of investments open to trustee funds (banks, insurance companies, pension funds) and this further constrained any development of alliance ownership. While 'patient' development money was hard to find, the financial system was a constraint on the diversification of the primary sector and the development of value-added processing. Through its lending preferences, support was concentrated on commodity production and independent farmers, leaving the processing sector largely to farmer cooperatives and foreign companies, both of whom had limited investment aspirations.

As large business organisations started to emerge in the 1960s and 1970s, ownership rapidly concentrated with a relatively few conglomerates (Le Heron, 1980). This was assisted by the trading of business ownership at its most extreme in the activity of takeover specialists such as Brierley Investments and similar companies. These investment companies have had an active management interest in their subsidiaries but often of a short-term nature to realise existing undervalued assets. Consequently, even though the sharemarket may have been small, Anglo Saxon conceptions of business ownership and management have been dominant. One analysis identified 515 mergers from 1977-82, for example, of which 21% were conglomerate in nature, 57% involved market concentration and 8% involved production chain integration (Pickford cited in Britton et al, 1993, p 57). Over a fifth of the mergers were the initiative of investment companies. The instability of business ownership has continued and sustained an economic structure sharply divided between a few large conglomerates and a mass of small enterprises (Hayward, 1996). The development of a system of business funding to promote the growth of independent, innovative enterprises continues to be seen as a major development constraint.

Incipient Corporatism

At various times since the 1960s, attempts were made to enlist labour and employer group participation in the identification of new economic development strategies. The first such initiative was the National Development Conference of 1969 which, although in itself judged as successful in the quality of its proposals, ultimately had little impact (Hawke, 1985). This and subsequent attempts to incorporate interest groups within national decision-making provide further evidence of the weakness and fragmentation of interest groups. They also perhaps suggest that an incipient corporatism reflected what should be possible in a small and exposed economy.

The 1969 conference was the single most comprehensive attempt to shift the balance of policy-making influence. It was linked to a National Development Council that was to coordinate the receipt of sector strategies prepared by representatives of interest groups. Economic circumstances changed in the 1970s and rapidly outdated the strategies. Whether this in itself caused the initiative to fail or whether it was the limited expertise and resources possessed by interest groups to sustain policy development is unclear. Their awareness that the initiative implied reduced direct access to government may also have been a contributing factor (Vowles, 1992, p 360). In 1973, the Labour government attempted to give the Employers' Federation and the Federation of Labour authority in industrial relations but neither organisation was able to obtain power over their memberships. A similar attempt by the next Labour government, through the 1987

Industrial Relations Act, had little greater impact although it did expose the difference between small and large employers over their support for national awards versus enterprise-level bargaining (Mabbett, 1995, p 171). Parallel with these efforts to integrate union organisation, employer groups moved to consolidate their policy-making networks, including the formation of a 'top tier' group of representatives from the main groups for the purposes of coordinating policy (Vowles, 1992; Vowles and Roper, 1997). This was carried through to proposals for amalgamation between the Employers' Federation, the Manufacturers' Federation and the Chamber of Commerce, but this significant step was stymied by "sectoral tensions" (Wanna, 1989, p 10).

Prior to its labour legislation, the newly elected fourth Labour government sponsored an 'economic summit' in September 1984 with the purpose of generating consensus over the direction of economic management. This initiative responded to a view within the Labour party that it was important to progress economic restructuring on the basis of consensus (Oliver, 1989). The advocates of this approach recognised that conditions were not auspicious for consensual decision-making as, for example, one former Cabinet Minister argued:

> It is not a failure to analyse the situation properly that is our problem. It is not even a failure to come up with the right solution ... The real failure has been the lack of awareness of the problem in the community at large, and the lack of willingness to co-operate to bring about a solution. And this all relates back to a deplorable lack of community spirit, and the decline of neighbourliness that are such obvious features of our society ... Selfishness stalks this land ... (Bassett, 1979, p 9)

The economic summit achieved some consensus amongst participants in terms of broad objectives, but this broke down as policy options became explicit (Dalziel, 1989). A notable feature was the cooperation amongst employer groups and the efforts of individual business organisations to strengthen their policy-making capacity, partly to counter the growing influence of the Business Roundtable that spoke for corporate business interests (Wanna, 1989, p 9). Nonetheless it was evident that neither the Federation of Labour or Employers' Federation had delegated authority

over their memberships. As expressed by the former Prime Minister David
Lange:

> We discovered very early on in the piece that you can't do
> trades there – because the parties have to impose the outcome
> on their members ... I tell you the government could honour
> a trade, but I am certain the union movement and Employers'
> Federation would not. (cited in Boston, 1986, p 9)

For those members of the government who opposed a corporatist
approach, the summit achieved its purpose in providing opportunity, as
they saw it, to blunt the power of lobby groups (see Douglas in Jesson,
1992, p 372). This perspective presented interest groups as merely
purveyors of vested interests pursuing sectional interests. Such a view
had some justification from the theory of unequal returns to lobbyists.
It is argued that protectionist lobbies are likely to form more easily than
free-trade lobbies, even where society is better off with free trade. The
gainers from trade protection are a small group receiving a large benefit,
while the losses are dispersed widely and are individually small. Although
those disadvantaged are in a numerical majority, the gainers have more
incentive to lobby intensively (Mabbett, 1995, p 15). This view has
taken successive governments away from further attempts at corporatist
strategies, although the recent shift to proportional representation has
introduced the possibility for new relationships between interest groups
and government to evolve.

Implications for Business Cooperation

The implications of the above discussion are that the New Zealand business
system has favoured individualistic organisation rather than inter-firm
cooperation. As discussed above, the propensity for business cooperation
is likely to increase in business systems distinguished by a high degree of
organisational commitment to their industry. Single compared with multi-
activity organisations have fewer options for managing risk and to this
extent they have a greater incentive to form alliances of one form or another
with other organisations. Activity specialisation has been linked to three
business system attributes:

(i)   long-term ownership interests;

(ii)   reciprocal employment relations that rely on trust between managers and employees; and

(iii) participation in industry associations.

The New Zealand business system has had one of these components but its impetus was offset by stronger components in the system.

Small enterprise is generally associated with activity specialisation and long-term ownership interests. When combined with family ownership, as in a good proportion of New Zealand's small business, it is also associated with a reluctance to share ownership rights. Moreover, the centralised award system and import protection provided protection from competition that seems likely to have reduced interest in other risk management strategies. Growth-orientated enterprises might be an exception, but they tended to be drawn into a less committed form of ownership. Other characteristics propitious for cooperation have been largely absent from the business system. The employment system and limits on union activity minimised the need for active engagement between employer and employees, although within small workplaces personal familiarity and the need for flexibility no doubt provided a sense of interdependence. Industry associations were fragmented and generally operated without active participation. A survey reported in the mid-1980s, for example, estimated that around 50% of employers were unaffiliated to any employer organisation and that few organisations even had a full-time secretary (Brosnan et al, 1985). The survey authors concluded that the absence of participation was probably not the result of apathy so much as the barriers to gaining influence in associations that tended to become the property of self-selected activists. In this context, there was little investment in collective resources and few controls on member behaviour that might have been an impetus for inter-firm cooperation. Similarly, a survey in the early 1990s of 44 industry associations found them to be unprepared for dealing with change, reactive and "bastions of the status quo" (Enderwick and Wilson, 1992). It was noted, for example, that few associations possessed a mission statement or other evidence of strategic capacity. Even so, most associations claimed that their role was to assist the competitiveness of their industry, citing five justifications for this work:

(i)   the small average size of members;

(ii)   the lack of resources and expertise within individual firms;

(iii)   the need for coordinated action;
(iv)   greater cost effectiveness of a collective approach over individual action; and
(v)   the need for a long-term strategy.

The survey was undertaken in the light of the Porter Project investigation that, among other recommendations, had included a role for industry associations in strengthening the competitiveness of companies. The implication of Enderwick and Wilson's (1992) investigation was that, while this was a responsibility, the associations recognised they were not equipped to perform it.

The direct impact of institutional legacies on the New Zealand business system remains to be verified. The consequence in terms of an uncooperative business culture may be inferred from a number of surveys undertaken in the early 1990s that indicated how most businesses operate in isolation from each other (Field et al, 1994). In the horticultural sector, a study of growers and processors in Hawke's Bay also found evidence of low cooperation within and between individual value chains (Perry et al, 1997). Public policy initiatives to promote various forms of business cooperation have gained increasing prominence over the last decade and have been motivated by a perceived need for intervention. Reviews of three such schemes in chapter 5 generally endorse the perception that business cooperation has been weak.

Doubts About Business Systems
There are a number of grounds on which objections might be made about business system perspectives. This section briefly comments upon three possible objections.

1.   One concern may be that the emphasis on national patterns of business behaviour gives too little scope for individual businesses to exercise their own strategic choices. Business system perspectives emphasise national characteristics because that is the dominant level of organisation for legal institutions, interest group coordination, resource markets and other influential attributes. On the other hand, it is recognised that business systems vary in their degree of integration as reflected in the extent to which key institutions and modes of behaviour are mutually re-enforcing. For example, it is evident that

important features of business ownership, the financial system and labour market are more integrated in Finland than they are in New Zealand. One indicator of this can be seen in the barriers that have faced industries in Finland that did not conform to the business practices developed in the dominant forestry sector (Lilija et al, 1992; Lilija and Tainio, 1996). New Zealand's business system has eschewed encompassing forms of organisation that ensure a comparable level of conformance, although it is still possible to identify some parameters within which most business has operated.

2. Some economists object to business system ideas on the grounds that, whatever the social conditions, competition requires that the most efficient arrangements are adopted and ultimately market forces bring uniform solutions. Economists have tried to use transaction cost analysis to explain differences in business organisation in this way (Williamson, 1994). Transaction cost economics has given particular attention to the circumstances under which organisations favour internal management (hierarchy), externalised transactions (market) or some form of hybrid arrangement (networks). This approach holds that economising on transaction costs is mainly responsible for the choice of one form of capitalist organisation over another. For example, transactions with uncertain outcomes that recur frequently and that require substantial specialisation of assets are expected to be internalised within management hierarchies. Exchanges that are straightforward, non-repetitive and require no transaction-specific investments are conversely expected to result in external market transactions. Such rules assume a neutral institutional environment and are based on stereotypical evaluations of the relative costs and benefits of alternative organisational forms (Granovetter, 1992). For example, transaction cost analysis has assumed that relationships in which supplier assets are specialised have lower transaction costs inside an organisation than between independent companies (Walker and Poppo, 1991). Creation of assets that are specific to a particular transaction are viewed as an invitation to opportunism: the firm investing in the assets has incurred a sunk cost and can be held to ransom by a customer exploiting this commitment; the customer, having no easy alternative source of supply, can be held to ransom by the supplier demanding higher prices. Examination of this issue from a business system perspective

has shown that the perception of risk associated with specific assets varies and so there is no universal solution as transaction cost analysis seeks to predict (Sako, 1992).

3. Business system analysis seeks to demonstrate that there are alternative ways of sustaining 'best practice'. This may be objected to from the perspective that the capacity to adjust to changing conditions needs to be considered as well as current performance. At the present time, for example, several of the distinctive business systems that Whitley (1992) assessed as alternative ways of sustaining best practice have since lost much of their dynamism (this includes Japanese *keiretsu*, Korean *chaebol* and German diversified quality production). In this regard it should be acknowledged that alliance ownership has been problematic for economic adjustment when combined with a lack of transparency in corporate governance and a willingness amongst banks to convert bad loans into equity. Lack of transparency has been particularly acute in Japan where the scale of accumulated debts has contributed to that country's prolonged recession (Masaki, 1998). These problems are associated with larger features of Japan's corporate laws. A more general weakness of credit-based financial systems may be their slowness in supporting new ventures as compared with equity-based systems. For these kinds of reasons, some claim that Anglo Saxon business methods are demonstrating their superiority in adapting to international competition and that globalisation means that business practice will increasingly conform to them (Fukuyama, 1992). For the present, such a claim remains conjecture as adaption takes place within the context of inherited structures and enduring values. Moreover, just as business conditions appear to have moved in favour of Anglo Saxon business methods, so they might change again. It has, for example, been argued that American capitalism thrives under conditions of technological uncertainty but has been less successful during periods of comparative technological stability (Kenney and Florida, 1993).

Conclusion

This chapter has argued that political institutions, welfare systems and economic structures created a distinctive New Zealand business system. A key aspect of this system was the dominant role of the state in economic management and business behaviour, which resulted in fragmented and weak interest associations. The centralised award system underscored the lack of engagement amongst economic actors reinforced by the absence of alliance forms of business ownership. Changes to the business system began to occur as non-traditional export producers, organised as large corporates and favouring 'flexible' employment relations, became more important. These producers believed that their interests were best served by rolling back the boundaries of the state both in trade and labour market regulation. This agenda was largely enacted and has had a major impact in reducing the sheltered sector of the economy and the viability of the institutions it had supported. The scale of government withdrawal from industry regulation and control has tended to encourage a view that the business environment has been entirely transformed. How far that view is justified is the subject of the next chapter. Meanwhile, it may be concluded that claims about shared trust and business cooperation are more credible in the case of the Nordic economies than for New Zealand. The retention of communal authority has provided business system conditions supportive of business integration in the Nordic economies, whereas institutional and political structures have provided little impetus to business cooperation in New Zealand.

4 • Shared Trust in New Zealand

The post-1984 focus on deregulation, privatisation and minimalist government involvement in the economy raises questions about the survival of the New Zealand business system described in the previous chapter. The changed scope of public sector regulation and control implies a significant transformation in the relationships between economic actors. In particular, the separation of the sheltered and competitive sectors has reduced across large parts of the manufacturing and service economy. The institutional fabric designed to suit the sheltered sector has disappeared, prompting and further enforcing the concentration of business activity in the competitive sector. Changes in the organisation of collective resources have prompted some forms of new provision, as in the area of industry training.

On the other hand, large parts of the business system have remained largely unchanged. The system of business finance and the market for business ownership has not been greatly modified. Deregulation of the financial market has affected the ownership of financial institutions but with little impact on the balance between credit and capital market reliance. Merger and acquisition activity generating instability in company ownership remains and may even have increased, although this might be an aspect of adjustment rather than an ongoing feature. Changes in the systems of skill acquisition and training have been made to promote employer involvement in training and assist the development of workplace-specific skills. Industry participation in training organisations has been strongest to protect small-business trades and overall it is not evident that competitive sector employers are changing relationships with their workforce. To some degree, labour market reform through the Employment Contracts Act 1991 has worked against support for such industry-supported training by facilitating employer use of external labour markets. The weakening of trade unions also produced by that legislation reduced a motivation for employer organisation. That context may change with the Employment Relations Act introduced in 2000, but meanwhile the scarcity of strong, industry-based employer groups has remained. The

64 • Shared Trust in New Zealand

Business Roundtable was an exception. It attained influence as the representative of major corporates, partly at the expense of longer established business groups. The cohesiveness of corporate interests tended to reduce during the 1990s and this somewhat diminished the Roundtable's influence (Cronin, 1997). Generally, direct lobbying of government by individual organisations remains an alternative to encompassing interest groups. Deregulation has been led by government and has taken place without reducing the legitimacy of the state to re-regulate. The shift to proportional representation has yet to bring any realignment of interest groups. That might take place if a dominant coalition partner emerged that threatened a long-term exclusion from influence of either employer or labour groups. If that were to occur, the excluded party would have a strong incentive to promote self-regulation with the group retaining influence.

Business system theory suggests that greater use of inter-firm alliances would occur if there is a marked shift in activity specialisation within the context of long-term ownership interests. As the above discussion indicates, neither of these stimuli have been directly affected by the changes in economic management. On the other hand, exposure to competition has required that many businesses develop new capabilities. To attain competitiveness there has been much advocacy of 'best practice' methods identified from internationally agreed definitions (Corbett, 1990, 1992, 1996, 1998; Vitalis and Walker, 1993; AMC/MAG, 1994). This guidance has focused on internal management issues, but the best practice recommended has also emphasised investment in improved relations with suppliers and customers. New Zealand's initial comparative performance was generally found lacking but there is some evidence that the shortfall may have reduced from the surveys coordinated by the Ministry of Commerce (AMC/MAG, 1994; Knuckey et al, 1999).

The latest Ministry of Commerce survey finds that there has been significant development of business networks that is judged to be "consistent with progress away from what used to be thought of as the traditional New Zealand introverted business culture" (Knuckey et al, 1999, p 88). That conclusion was based on responses from 1173 manufacturing establishments and survey results indicating, for example, that 63% of large firms (40 or more FTE employees) work quite or very closely with suppliers on product development and 53% in the case of process improvement (corresponding figures for medium-sized firms [10-39.5 FTE employees] were 52% and 42% respectively). The proportion reporting that they worked quite or very closely with customers on product development was 72% and 70% for large and medium-sized firms respectively. Such figures, which the survey noted were a large increase over the earlier survey (AMC/MAG, 1994), suggest that businesses increasingly operate within highly integrated production chains linking input suppliers to end buyers.

While production chain integration is only one form of cooperation, if the interpretation of the best practice survey evidence is correct it suggests either that the expected stimuli to business cooperation identified in business system theory are incomplete (or perhaps wrongly specified) or that the transformation from the sheltered to the competitive sector has propelled change in a particularly dramatic way. It was beyond the scope of the best practice investigation to examine the form or precise significance of the cooperative relationships it counted. It is possible that what is being reported often represents modest changes in purchasing and sales strategies rather than shifts to 'boundary crossing' organisational forms. The experience of various policy initiatives that have sought to promote business cooperation (see chapter 5) certainly suggests that less radical change has taken place than is indicated in the best practice survey. In this context there is still justification for exploring the environment for cooperation and how far impediments exist from the inherited patterns of business behaviour. This chapter examines these issues through the findings of a survey that examined perceptions about the existence of shared trust and the environment for business cooperation.

Measuring Shared Trust

The originators of shared trust offer no indicators from which to gauge its presence but some may be inferred from their description of the concept. Of central concern is the extent of business cooperation. This is broadly conceived to include an absence of underhand behaviour and concern that other parties will take advantage of information extended to them on trust. Formal cooperation in the form of resource sharing, and participation in industry associations or alliances would thus not capture the full scope of what is envisaged. Qualitatively it implies measurement of business managers' assessment of five aspects of their environment.

• The extent to which business managers believe that they share similar

backgrounds and values with other managers in related businesses.
* The significance of any commonality of backgrounds and values amongst business managers in facilitating cooperation.
* The extent of disadvantage in being judged an outsider or maverick by other business managers and whether or not the risk of being so judged acts to curb behaviour.
* The willingness of business managers to support collective informal sanctions against businesses that break trust and the likelihood of such sanctions deterring cheating or opportunism.
* The extent to which the trust extended to managers depends on the length and nature of previous working experience with that manager, as compared with being equally present in relations with familiar and new trading partners.

As well as the perceptions of managers it is possible to suggest a number of quantitative indicators of shared trust. These data can help verify qualitative judgements, although in practice it may be hard to obtain or interpret such data.

1. The number of business organisations in industries under study and their individual shares of total output test the feasibility of high familiarity amongst managers and the equality of relations. Shared trust assumes that a 'restricted' number of players in any industry facilitates the informal surveillance of business behaviour, the effectiveness of which is expected to lower barriers to cooperation. A complication is that the balance of large and small firms in an industry, and their dependencies on a single sector, affect the extent of attachment and interest in relationships with other industry participants (Perry, 1995; Uriu, 1996). Consequently, even if there was an agreed threshold of the number of participants imposing a constraint on industry cohesion, interpretation of participation data is not straightforward.

2. The extent of common backgrounds can be examined from participation records in education and training establishments and subsequent career biographies. This source of evidence was drawn on by Maskell et al (1998, p 171) to show, for example, how influential members of one development pair (the Swedish Power Board and ASEA, a private company) included several that had

graduated together. Similarly, the participation of individual managers in industry and social organisations can be examined to identify the existence of opportunity for informal and formal interaction. Of course, raw membership data may not reflect actual participation which is one problem in interpreting such records.

3. Mapping the geographical clustering of industry participants is an indicator of the ease of face-to-face and informal interaction. Ease of personal interaction is envisaged as a further influence that helps to build shared trust, but the assumption that physical proximity stimulates interaction is questionable. Close neighbours need not interact and with modern technology there need not be barriers to sustaining long distance communication.

4. The existence of industry associations, the extent of delegated authority obtained by such associations and the level of participation from their potential membership are relevant to the assessment of shared trust. The originators of the concept refer to such participation as one of the mechanisms for building interaction and commitment to the collective well-being of their industry. Once again some insight is obtained from participation levels but ideally this is supplemented by investigation of actual involvement and operation of the association.

Does Shared Trust Exist in New Zealand?

It has been suggested in previous chapters that claims about the role of shared trust are more credible in the context of the Nordic small economies than New Zealand. To examine this proposition, a survey was undertaken to examine what business advisors and managers judge to be the status of shared trust. Resources permitted no more than a preliminary investigation to be undertaken relying on the qualitative indicators identified in the previous section. The evidence collected permits some conclusions to be drawn but perhaps more importantly it may lead others to investigate the climate for cooperation.

The survey sought informed opinions by eliciting responses from persons with direct experience of business cooperation, either as a promoter, coordinator or participant. The promoters and coordinators (56 in total) were either an official from Trade New Zealand (10), a manager of an industry training organisation (28) or a coordinator of an industry association (18). Seeking the views of these persons maximised the scope of a small-scale investigation by contacting persons with industry-wide experience. The participants selected for the survey were business managers who had joined some form of industry or locality-based group. A total of 127 business managers was contacted of whom 46.5% returned a completed response. This sample was constrained by the need to rely on a publicly available membership list of the group surveyed, but this still enabled the coverage of a range of different industries.[1] Responses were collected through a postal survey (85 responses) and in the context of personal interviews (30 responses). The latter enabled the perceptions to be explained and verified with specific experiences, and the consistency with other responses may be seen to add some confidence to the overall responses. The material gathered in the interviews is mainly used in the review of public policy initiatives (chapter 5, but some comments directly linked to shared trust are included with the survey results.

The small samples, drawn from those with an interest in encouraging support for business cooperation, are clearly a constraint on interpreting the data. The broad consistency in the responses obtained from promoters/coordinators and business managers may give some weight to the findings, particularly as the business managers included both lapsed and ongoing group participants whose views might vary about the need for barriers to cooperation. The survey included assessments of four indicators of shared trust, namely:

(i)   the perceived scope for cooperation;
(ii)   the extent to which business managers share similar backgrounds and values;
(iii)   the significance of shared backgrounds and values for facilitating cooperation;
(iv)   the perceived disadvantage of being an outsider or maverick; and
(v)   other business characteristics affecting cooperation and trust.

Scope for Cooperation

The majority of respondents agree that business performance is enhanced through cooperation with other businesses and that there is too little business cooperation in New Zealand (Table 4.1). Perhaps not surprisingly, promoters/coordinators of cooperation most frequently agreed that there is too little cooperation but almost three-quarters of business managers agreed that this was so too. Compared with the Nordic interpretation that smallness assists cooperation, 40% of business managers believed that it had the opposite effect by reducing the opportunity for cooperation. For the majority of respondents, it would appear that other constraints are limiting cooperation.

Table 4.1 Support for Cooperation

	A.	B.	C.	D.	E.
Business performance in relation to such issues as sales volume, penetrating new markets, production efficiency and innovation is improved when participating in a cooperative relationship with other firms.					
Business managers[1]	50.8	44.1	—	1.7	3.4
Coordinators[2]	48.2	48.2	—	—	3.6
There is too little business cooperation in New Zealand.					
Business managers	33.9	40.7	20.3	—	5.1
Coordinators	30.4	53.6	10.7	3.6	1.8
There are not sufficient cooperative opportunities in a small economy such as New Zealand for it to be an important part of the business scene.					
Business managers	5.1	33.9	30.5	30.5	—
Coordinators	10.7	8.9	19.6	57.1	3.6

A=Strongly agree; B=Somewhat agree; C=Somewhat disagree; D=Strongly disagree; E=Don't know
1 – percentage of respondents, n = 59
2 – percentage of respondents, n = 56

The premise behind the significance of shared trust is that the culture affecting business norms is comparatively homogeneous in a small compared with a large country. With respect to the dominant population of European-settler descent, there is a lack of significant regional differentiation in, for example, religion, ethnic affiliations and social status that suggests this condition holds for New Zealand. Respondents tend to support this view in so far as agreeing that there is "personal familiarity, common background and shared culture" amongst business managers

(Table 4.2). Where opportunities for cooperation exist, most respondents believed that this perceived commonality makes business cooperation relatively easy to establish, although promoters/coordinators are less convinced that this is the case than are business managers. On the other hand, the majority of all respondents agree that the "the business culture has given little support for cooperation". This suggests that while personal familiarity may assist cooperation it is not sufficient to stimulate cooperation. Similarly, around two-thirds of respondents do not believe

Table 4.2 Business Culture and Cooperation

	A.	B.	C.	D.	E.
There is a high degree of personal familiarity, common background and shared culture amongst business owners and managers in New Zealand.					
Business managers[1]	33.9	49.1	8.5	3.4	5.1
Coordinators[2]	28.6	48.2	8.9	8.9	5.3
New Zealand's business culture has given little support for cooperation between firms.					
Business managers	23.7	32.2	32.2	8.5	3.4
Coordinators	26.8	35.7	25.0	10.7	1.8
The personal familiarity, common background and shared culture amongst business owners and managers mean that where opportunities exist business cooperation is relatively easy to establish.					
Business managers	20.3	52.6	22.0	1.7	3.4
Coordinators	14.3	44.6	26.8	8.9	5.3
Trust amongst business owners and managers is high irrespective of how long they have worked with each other.					
Business managers	—	35.6	47.4	13.6	3.4
Coordinators	5.3	12.5	53.6	17.8	10.7

A=Strongly agree; B=Somewhat agree; C=Somewhat disagree; D=Strongly disagree; E=Don't know
1 – percentage of respondents, n = 59
2 – percentage of respondents, n = 56

that trust between business managers exists irrespective of the extent of their work experience with each other. The perceived need to develop trust through working experience contrasts with the Nordic expectation that the 'default relationship' between businesses tends to be one of trust. That quality is central to the existence of shared trust. It is claimed to lower the effort required to obtain close ties between business managers. As a consequence it should be easier to break ties as needs change, avoiding fixed relations that can become a burden when markets and technologies change.

Business managers and promoters/coordinators differ in their perception of the constraint on cooperation imposed by the availability of opportunities versus the willingness to cooperate (Table 4.3). Business managers are evenly divided on whether business willingness or opportunity is the greater constraint on cooperation; promoters/coordinators are more inclined to perceive 'willingness' as the larger constraint than 'opportunity'. When attitudes to cooperation are counterpoised with "practical considerations, ... opportunities or the time and effort to establish ties", managers and coordinators agree strongly that attitudes are the greater

Table 4.3 Opportunity or Attitude

	A.	B.	C.	D.	E.
Lack of business opportunity or need is a greater constraint on participation in business cooperation than the willingness of business owners and managers to cooperate.					
Business managers[1]	5.1	37.3	25.4	27.1	5.1
Coordinators[2]	1.8	19.6	41.1	33.9	3.6
Attitudes amongst business owners and managers are a greater barrier to business cooperation than practical considerations such as the availability of cooperative opportunities or the time and effort to establish ties.					
Business managers	32.2	42.4	18.6	6.8	—
Coordinators	35.7	46.4	14.3	1.8	1.8

A=Strongly agree; B=Somewhat agree; C=Somewhat disagree; D=Strongly disagree; E=Don't know
1 – percentage of respondents, n = 59
2 – percentage of respondents, n = 56

constraint, although once again this view is most frequent amongst coordinators. Across these indicators there is a consistent suggestion that attitudes rather than practical concerns deter cooperation. This is consistent with support expressed for cooperation and the belief that cooperation is comparatively easy to establish given the common values amongst managers. It would appear, therefore, that the negative attitudes may be connected to the perceived risks of entering cooperative relations.

One respondent interviewed indicated from his own experience some of his ambivalent attitudes to and uses of trust. He explained that while he had close contact with the managers of a business located nearby, he had little contact with other managers in the industry, including some who were also near neighbours. Having at least one 'friendly' company was felt to be important because there was little direct contact with other members of the industry. Although there is an industry association, the manager took no active part in it, characterising it as being too much under the control of one business "that could not be trusted". The business with whom they did cooperate gave opportunity to coordinate investment in new equipment, although this was mainly limited to informing each other of their intentions rather than resource sharing. This mutual support had developed over many years and was helped, it was suggested, by family friendships going back to school days.

Business Trust

The responses discussed above suggest that trust amongst business managers is dependent on working relationships rather than a natural feature of the business system. The ability to sanction mavericks is expected to sustain shared trust in a small economy. This capacity is linked to the existence of generally accepted norms of business behaviour and the high transparency of transactions in a small community. The survey responses provide a mixed assessment of the perceived strength of such enforcement mechanisms.

More than three-quarters of business managers and over two-thirds of coordinators believe that "businesses that break trust ... would find it hard to survive" (Table 4.4). Less support is given for the proposition that 'insiders' are concerned about being excluded from 'the group' to the extent that it restrains them from using insider knowledge to the disadvantage of other members. With respect to insider behaviour, the majority 'somewhat agree' rather than 'strongly agree' with the proposition that the risk of

Table 4.4 Trust and Outsider Behaviour

	A.	B.	C.	D.	E.
Businesses that break trust with other businesses would find it hard to survive.					
Business managers[1]	49.1	27.2	22.0	—	1.7
Coordinators[2]	33.9	33.9	25.0	3.6	3.6
Insiders do not exploit cooperation for individual gain, to the disadvantage of other members, because it would result in their exclusion from the group.					
Business managers	13.6	52.5	18.6	3.4	11.8
Coordinators	7.1	46.4	23.2	1.8	21.4
Outsider firms seeking to undermine or free ride on the investment of others are a significant problem.					
Business managers	15.2	40.7	18.6	10.2	15.2
Coordinators	10.7	33.9	30.4	3.6	21.4

A=Strongly agree; B=Somewhat agree; C=Somewhat disagree; D=Strongly disagree; E=Don't know
1 – percentage of respondents, n = 59
2 – percentage of respondents, n = 56

expulsion from 'the group' acts to prevent disruption by mavericks. A particularly large share of business respondents indicates that while they believe that trust breaking would make business survival hard, they are less certain that exclusion is a threat sufficient to moderate behaviour. Confidence that there is a trust-enforcing environment reduces further in respect of the problem presented by outsiders to cooperation. Both business managers and coordinators indicate that outsiders pose a significant problem to cooperation, either by seeking to undermine initiatives that they are not a party to or by free riding on the project's investment. This perception is more strongly held by business managers than coordinators. The greater sensitivity to outsider disruption amongst business managers than coordinators may reflect the stronger interest that managers have in preserving the value of their investment in cooperation.

A comparatively large proportion of respondents declined to judge the existence of insider and outsider risks. This indecision reflects the lack of experience with disruptive behaviour which makes it hard for respondents to judge whether the problem exists and the response it would bring. Lack of direct experience may be indicative of the low incidence of such problems, although the uncertainty expressed suggests that disruption is at least recognised as a possibility. Similarly the value of the judgements that were offered depends on the interpretation of the experience that they have had.

In the questionnaire, a business manager who indicated that a firm breaking trust would survive unaffected based this on his experience of a competitor. This competitor had sought to 'grab' market share through aggressive pricing. This had disrupted the established industry norms and, it was claimed, had resulted in the competitor subsequently going bankrupt with large unpaid debts to subcontractors in the industry. The business owner re-entered the industry partly, it is suggested, using assets taken out of his original business prior to its bankruptcy. The respondent noted that an initial informal industry decision to shun the business rapidly broke down. The new operation continues to operate, from which the respondent concluded that breaking trust does not threaten survival. In contrast, a fishing industry respondent believed that breaking trust would make it hard to survive and that consequently trust was respected. In this sector, it was suggested that the sharing of resources, including fishing vessels, and knowledge of each others' catches (through the quota system) made business relations transparent and ensured that trust was respected.

Business Characteristics and Cooperation
Stability of business ownership and employment are necessary for sustaining significant inter-firm cooperation. Around three quarters of business managers and coordinators agreed that changes in personnel and company ownership frequently disrupt business relations (Table 4.5). This perception is consistent with the description of the business system given in chapter 3. An expected outcome of the market forms of business ownership and comparatively uncommitted relationship between employers and employees is a high turnover of personnel. This turnover becomes a constraint on cooperation to the extent that relations between businesses involve connection and understanding between individuals in those organisations. Other widely perceived barriers to cooperation were:

- Over two-thirds of business managers agree that large companies were disinterested in mutual development opportunities with small firms. Coordinators are less persuaded that large firms are dismissive of cooperation with small firms but the majority share the opinion of most managers.

- A majority of business managers and coordinators agree that foreign companies are less inclined to cooperate than local businesses, although the barriers here seem to be marginally less than those created by large-firm attitudes.

Consistent with the assessment of big-firm attitudes, most business managers believe that cooperation is greatest amongst firms of similar size and experience. Coordinators are once again fairly evenly dispersed in their assessment of this issue but with a small majority agreeing with the assessment of business managers. A comparatively large number of respondents declined to comment on the perceived willingness of foreign companies to cooperate, reflecting the lack of experience in seeking cooperation with foreign companies. Overall, there is no evidence of absolute barriers to cooperation with either large or foreign companies but the mixed perceptions collected in the survey do illustrate how industry ownership characteristics can affect the scope of shared trust.

As discussed in the previous chapter, there has been an absence of strong encompassing organisations and in this context cross-industry cooperation has been left largely to the initiative of individual organisations. Survey respondents predominantly agree that industry associations still give a low priority to cross industry cooperation. On the other hand, the majority of respondents disagree that business cooperation is more likely to "defend entitlements or markets than it is to develop new projects". Nonetheless, over a third of business managers and coordinators did accept this conservative focus of cooperation, reinforcing other judgements suggesting that there is too little business cooperation.

Summary

The survey suggests that personal familiarity and shared culture are judged to exist and that this makes cooperation relatively easy. Even so the business culture is judged by most to have been unsupportive of cooperation. Unlike the claim in Nordic economies, trust between business partners comes mainly from the experience of individual business relations rather than

Table 4.5 Business relations

	A.	B.	C.	D.	E.
Changes in personnel or ownership of member organisations frequently disrupt business relations.					
Business managers[1]	13.6	64.4	11.8	5.1	5.1
Coordinators[2]	19.6	53.6	17.8	3.6	5.3
For the big players, mutual development opportunities with smaller firms are generally not part of their agenda.					
Business managers	33.9	35.6	20.3	6.8	3.4
Coordinators	17.8	32.1	39.3	7.1	3.6
Cooperation is greatest amongst firms of similar size and experience.					
Business managers	25.4	35.6	20.3	6.8	3.4
Coordinators	10.7	42.8	28.6	12.5	5.3
Foreign-owned businesses are less inclined to support cooperation than New Zealand organisations.					
Business managers	11.8	35.6	23.7	10.2	18.6
Coordinators	10.7	33.9	17.8	12.5	25.0
Industry associations protect the interests of their members with little regard to the potential for cooperation between different industries.					
Business managers	11.8	44.1	28.8	10.2	5.1
Coordinators	10.7	41.1	26.8	19.6	1.8
Business cooperation is more likely to defend existing entitlements or markets than it is to develop new projects.					
Business managers	10.2	27.1	42.4	18.6	1.7
Coordinators	5.3	30.4	35.7	25.0	3.6

A=Strongly agree; B=Somewhat agree; C=Somewhat disagree; D=Strongly disagree; E=Don't know
1 – percentage of respondents, n = 59

being the result of societal cohesion. A further gap in the environment for shared trust appears to be the absence of collective solidarity against mavericks. The consequence of that lack of enforcement is that breaking trust may go unpunished and this may reduce the willingness to cooperate. The significance of these results alone is hard to judge. There are no comparative data from the Nordic economies to demonstrate that there are real differences with the New Zealand business environment. Nor does the survey indicate anything about the incidence of problems amongst growth-orientated versus less ambitious enterprises. Nonetheless it may be a cause of concern that a distinctive opportunity for a small economy, arising from its comparative cultural homogeneity, small business communities and density of personal contact networks, appears not to be facilitating business cooperation.

Endnote

1. The business managers were selected from both lapsed and continuing cooperative initiatives that involved one of the following activities: manufacturing of wood products, plastics, personal care products; house design and construction; construction-linked engineering services; earthquake engineering technology and risk management services.

5 • Promoting Business Cooperation

The discussion so far has made two main points about small industrial countries: first, that their industries can be advantaged by a high degree of trust and cooperation, arising from personal familiarity, common values and the transparency of small-country business communities; and, second, that New Zealand's business system has evolved differently to that of Nordic small economies where the claims about the significance of shared trust have been developed. In particular, it has been argued that the weak development of communal authority has constrained the use of shared trust and that this has militated against business cooperation. That explanation remains speculative but the outcome in terms of an absence of business cooperation may be less controversial as the weakness and fragmentation of industry associations have been drawn attention to in several studies. As well, the survey evidence reported in the previous chapter has provided some contemporary support for the proposition that shared trust is not providing the impetus to business cooperation that might be expected in a small country. Based on these two observations, this chapter comments on recent efforts to promote business cooperation in New Zealand.

In contrast to the government's overall withdrawal from industry assistance, the 1990s witnessed much activity designed to promote 'business networks'. Reviewing these efforts provides another perspective on the state of business cooperation, as well as providing guidance on appropriate types of future intervention.

This chapter, therefore, has a dual purpose: first, to examine what existing experience in promoting business cooperation says about the business environment; and second, to identify future strategies for assisting business cooperation based on the impacts of past intervention. Much of the past effort to strengthen business cooperation was the initiative of Trade New Zealand. They sought to encourage a 'network' approach to export development. This effort has taken three main forms which are examined in this chapter in the sequence in which they arose, namely:

(i)   industry groups;
(ii)   hard business networks; and
(iii) clusters.

In addition, the chapter comments on the relationship between shared trust and social capital since the latter has been identified as an emerging policy area that is closely linked to the goal of encouraging business cooperation. The recommendations for future intervention are the subject of the next chapter.

Joint Action Groups

Active industry associations are a feature of Nordic small industrial countries that have been claimed to be a contributor to their high degree of shared trust (Maskell, 1998). Industry associations can promote shared trust by providing opportunities for formal and informal interaction, including participation in collective industry projects, as well as by raising the costs of being an 'outsider' where membership of the association confers significant benefits. Membership of industry associations has been high in New Zealand but it would appear without similar impact in encouraging business cooperation. For example, a survey conducted in the light of the Porter Project (Crocombe et al, 1991) suggestion that competitive advantage is partly created through industry groups found that industry associations were ill prepared for this task (Enderwick and Wilson, 1992). The joint action group (JAG) programme was set up in response to this perceived weakness as well as specific guidance from the Porter Project on opportunities in a number of industries. The basic concept was not original. Trade New Zealand (or the Market Development Board as it was originally) had previously delivered export assistance to groups in its efforts to accelerate export capacity following the trade agreements with Australia in the early 1980s.

Trade New Zealand encouraged businesses to join JAGs by giving them priority in the allocation of export assistance and through part-funding of the group's overheads. Even without these inducements, they envisaged that support for membership would be high because of the benefits to be obtained from a group approach to export market promotion. This had particular relevance for new markets where there was a need for basic information gathering and generic promotional and research activity to raise awareness of New Zealand products or services. As well, pooled marketing budgets could maximise the impact of individual resources as through a joint trade stand at an exhibition or shared marketing agents. It was also hoped that the JAGs would foster a 'NZ Inc' outlook whereby there would be mutual support amongst exporters recognising their shared goal of strengthening New Zealand's business community.

The 'Stretching for Growth' project, in which Trade New Zealand sought to goad export ambition, reiterated that export support "can be more effectively delivered to collectives of businesses rather than to individual businesses" (Trade New Zealand, 1996, p 7). JAGs remained the cornerstone of this collective approach until 1999 when support shifted to 'export networks'. The new programme still encourages businesses to work cooperatively but an export network might be a one-off project, such as a single overseas marketing trip. Participation in an export network does not require membership of an ongoing group, although it is recognised that network projects are likely to be encouraged by joint participation in some form of larger group.

At the peak of the programme in the mid-1990s, over 30 JAGs were active (Perry, 1995). In most cases, activity or membership or both reduced after an initial period of enthusiasm. Around 20 groups have survived the withdrawal of Trade New Zealand funding for group coordinators in 1999. A small number of these survivors have the status of 'industry groups': these include the New Zealand Marine Export Group (Marex), the Pine Manufacturers Association and the New Zealand Organic Products Exporters Group (OPEG). These three groups remained active, have at least a part-time executive staff and are encompassing of their potential membership. Another cluster of JAGs are those that were an offshoot of an established industry association and which have been absorbed back into that association or have continued as a separate group with their parent association's sponsorship. The North Asia Group JAG, for example, was a project of the Forest Owners Association and now continues, although in a slightly different form, through Wood New Zealand (a project promoted by the New Zealand Forest Industry Council, of which the Forest Owners Association are members). The New Zealand Wine Guild JAG was established for marketing in the UK when few members of the New Zealand Wine Institute supplied this market. This work is now part of the larger activity of the Wine Institute after the winding up of the Wine Guild. For these former JAGs, activity has continued with the benefit of the resources provided by compulsory levies or corporate members prepared to pay high membership fees as well as the linkage to a larger association.

Other surviving groups have varying levels of activity. Those that remain most active have the support of a part-time coordinator funded by the group. Foodsystems New Zealand is such a group which brings together engineering companies specialising in the manufacture of processing equipment. It continues with around 14 members compared with a peak of over 40. Other groups continue without a coordinator and typically with much reduced activity compared with previous years. Some describe themselves as an occasional 'coffee club'. The collective identity is retained to pick up activity from past projects and to maintain the links that have been made, as well as in case the JAG programme is revitalised in some form. The reduced activity following the loss of financial support from Trade New Zealand attracts different interpretations.

Government judges the performance of Trade New Zealand mainly according to its direct impact on foreign exchange earnings. On that indicator, JAGs were of declining utility to the agency for four main reasons. First, JAGs had tended to become less inclusive of their industry than had been the original intention. This made it hard to justify the priority in export assistance given to JAG members over outsiders. Second, a large proportion of resources (perhaps a third or more) was being diverted into group management and domestic activities rather than export development, a problem accentuated by the multiplication of small groups. Fragmentation of groups, each with their own fees and obligations, potentially required diversified organisations to participate in several groups and this tended to further weaken interest from some potential members. Third, there was much variability between groups in the relative financial inputs from Trade New Zealand and group members, partly reflected in large differences in their membership fees. This lack of consistency suggested weak commitment in some groups or a lack of consistent treatment, which raised public accountability issues for Trade New Zealand. Four, there was little interaction between JAGs which was seen as another example of the impediments to achieving a wide and effective distribution of export assistance.

Based on interviews with a sample of former JAG participants (see Appendix), there are differing judgements on the appropriateness of the change in Trade New Zealand support. Some recognise that their group was not particularly effective, others argue that its activities justified some ongoing financial support. Two broad points were made as well as reference to their individual activities:

- Membership shrinkage was a necessary process of identifying a group of businesses with common interests that could cooperate in shared export markets. This might have involved reconciling which competitors remained in the group and which exited, a problem that particularly arose with contract-based construction and engineering activities. In other cases, activity and market specialisation was needed to enable productive cooperation as in the emergence of sub-groups within the building industry export group (see below).
- A neutral coordinator and a comparatively modest membership subscription had often been a key to a group's progress. These attributes, made possible by Trade New Zealand support, had prevented 'capture' by self-interested members and enabled motivated participants to become advocates for the group. It was explained that without external support two concerns would have stymied lead firms emerging. First, as group activists potentially become highly knowledgeable about the position of individual members, suspicion as to their motive produces resistance to join. Second, prior experience with their established trade association was often of groups that were perceived to operate as the 'fiefdoms' of one or two companies, and this shaped expectations as to how their own activity in the JAG might be interpreted. The reality of these claims requires investigation but they are consistent with past research evidence of membership conflicts within established industry associations (Brosnan et al, 1985).

While not a final resolution of the contrasting interpretations, in the absence of any full evaluation of the programme yet being completed, several aspects of the programme and its reform can be pointed to as evidence of its usefulness.

Early Impact
A review of JAG activity completed in 1994 found that many benefits were being obtained (Perry, 1995). A general pattern was for groups to appoint a full- or part-time coordinator, prepare an industry capability profile for group publicity, and to develop a structured programme of

activities designed to help members gain access to selected overseas markets and make customer contacts. Discussion with coordinators revealed much enthusiasm, a large measure of industry support and also a high degree of novelty in the experience of individual companies working together. Some experienced exporters did support projects that most directly benefited new-to-exporting firms, perhaps most strongly in the case of the apparel and textile group. At the same time, there were indications that a willingness to cooperate was not always the motive for participation.

Early experience included cases where key industry participants would not join groups, preferring not to share their export knowledge and accusations that some outsiders were actively seeking to disrupt group initiatives. Established exporters sometimes rejected projects in markets that they already operated in, making it hard to maintain a programme of activities of interest to all members (the apparel and textile group being an exception). Group cohesion was easier in cases where few members were established exporters. Experienced exporters preferred to work with like organisations rather than mentor-aspiring exporters. They sought confidence of comparable commitment, ability and potential rewards. Attempts to promote cross-sector JAGs were unsuccessful and in some cases existing exporters formed a JAG to protect their established strategies from new entrants that they feared might have priorities that conflicted with their own.

Membership Rationalisation

The general pattern, as noted above, was that groups tended to fragment into smaller and more specialised groups than at the outset. As well as reflecting better understanding of the scope of synergies, which perhaps can only be obtained through experience, membership rationalisation reflected conflicts between participants. In contract-based groups, such as construction and engineering, competing contractors would typically not work together. In this context, groups had first to resolve who remained inside and who left the group. The changing participation has also to be considered against the context in which the programme was introduced.

The programme started post-deregulation as increasing numbers of organisations were facing up to the new economic environment and the need to become an exporter. Companies joined a group to explore opportunities and identify their target markets. Typical participants were small companies with limited capacity and ambition. They benefited from undertaking market exploration collectively, but once they had resolved their market priorities and had established customer contacts, the group could cease to be so important to them. Groups comprising a few experienced exporters and many small inexperienced companies, as in the case of the apparel and textile export group, lost momentum as the goodwill of the larger exporters declined and smaller exporters fulfilled their expansion goals.

These developments are partly illustrated with the case of the Building Industry Export Group. The original supporters of the group had researched its need and organisation prior to setting up the JAG. Their research involved both a survey of potential members and reviews of other JAGs to identify 'success factors'. Activity commenced with a successful joint trade show in Fiji. The group grew to around 50 members, including a good representation of building products manufacturers and construction companies. It appointed a full-time coordinator in 1993. Responding to member preferences, the Australian and Southeast Asian markets were selected as the initial targets for promotion. Despite initial declarations of interest, the Australian programme attracted little support despite members having identified this as a priority market. Two explanations for the lack of participation became apparent:

(i)   Australia was seen as an extension of the domestic market, with companies either already operating there or preferring to work alone in this market; and

(ii) a New Zealand identity was not seen as an advantage in Australia and, to the extent that the group was about strengthening this identity, it was viewed as a disadvantage.

In Southeast Asia, participation reduced as it became evident that the region had to be addressed as separate national markets. Once individual countries were targeted, the group fragmented with, for example, around six companies joining a mission to Vietnam. After several years the group had effectively become a dozen or more subgroups, based on a sector or geographic market focus. With encouragement from Trade New Zealand, which at that stage wanted to increase the number of JAGs, some subgroups became JAGs in their own right (including airport technologies, foodsystems and kitset homes). This trend suited specialists, but for multi-activity companies it resulted in a loss of attachment to any single group, and reduced sector-wide activity. With the loss of support from the original group, it was refashioned as 'Constructive Solutions'. This collective identity was to provide a single point of contact for overseas customers. Over 20 companies joined this initiative. Members were mainly specialist companies, resolving the difficulties of gaining agreement between direct competitors that had been a further constraint on the original group. Even so, with varying degrees of commitment and little consistent participation, the efforts of the coordinator were essential in sustaining a programme of activities. Within individual projects, much goodwill and mutual support amongst participants was said to be evident. On the other hand, from Trade New Zealand's perspective, too little of their support was being devoted to actual export promotion as compared with the effort invested in maintaining membership. After Trade New Zealand funding was withdrawn, 27 members agreed to maintain the group through an annual fee. The annual subscription will enable the coordinator, now part time, to do little more than follow up on any impact from past promotion. New activity will depend on user-pays funding and the initiative of the coordinator to promote individual projects.

Encompassing Groups

There are a number of groups that have retained broad support and that continue to be active with reduced support from Trade New Zealand. Amongst these are the three groups referred to above (Marex, the Pine Manufactures Association and OPEG) and Defence Technologies. Generally they are linked to new industries, or at least to industries that are new to exporting so that there is opportunity to address generic marketing issues as well as other specific influences encouraging cooperation. In the case of Defence Technologies, for example, the group has facilitated access to the Defence Force and Ministry of Defence and other learning opportunities in dealing with defence procurement agencies. The pine group is partly valued for its assistance on researching benchmark prices in the USA, the main new export market for member products which are typically standard items sold at uniform prices. Marine and organics have the advantage of being in expanding industries.

Promoting Export Networks

Under its new 'export networks' scheme, Trade New Zealand has increased access to its export assistance and is concentrating its limited funds directly on export promotion projects. It has been recognised that help may be needed to maintain opportunity for businesses to come together to identify joint opportunities. To address that need, the amalgamation of the JAGs into three broad sector-based associations ('mega-JAGs') was considered. Economies in administration costs and ongoing contact amongst business managers would have been obtained but access to export assistance would not have widened as far as under the new scheme. Instead, it is proposed to hold sector-based gatherings several times a year. These may combine education seminars on export issues with opportunities for business networking and are being considered to fill any gap left from the reduced activity of JAGs. As well, Trade New Zealand promotes export networks to industry associations, including surviving JAGs, and so one possibility is that they might be encouraged to take on a larger role in export development than they have provided traditionally. Alternatively, and as many in the former JAG programme hope, it might be necessary to revive the mega JAG proposal to maintain a flow of good quality export network projects.

Hard Networks
The strengthening of industry associations provides an indirect way of encouraging business cooperation. The association promotes collective activities and shared commitments that prospective members may or may not join. Directly promoting business alliances and joint ventures may be viewed as a more secure strategy than support to associations. This viewpoint was partly the influence behind a second Trade New Zealand programme, launched in late 1994, to encourage the formation of 'hard networks'. These were envisaged as groupings, typically of from four to six companies with unrealised export ambition and a willingness to work together. To lock-in the network and provide certainty to participants, individual networks were to be formalised with contractual ties. Independent business consultants ('brokers') were appointed to take the initiative in bringing firms together and to assist the implementation of network projects.

The specific idea for the programme came from the Danish Technological Institute (DTI), which had administered a similar scheme in Denmark and which undertook the feasibility study for its introduction to New Zealand (DTI, 1994). With the DTI's endorsement and awareness that other countries including Australia were also moving to copy the initiative, Trade New Zealand adapted the original model and reported positively on its potential following a pilot programme in Canterbury (Ffowcs Williams, 1996).

There has been no formal evaluation of the programme following its cessation in 1999. Late in the programme it was reported that 95 networks were in formation (Healy, 1997). Although subsidies to participants were modest, especially compared with the original Danish programme, they were concentrated at the feasibility investigation stage. The initial impact was not, therefore, a good indicator of commitment and viability. Probably few, if any, sustainable business groups of any significance resulted. It had been thought that private sector brokers, working on a part-time basis, would be more effective than using public officials, as occurred in Denmark. In practice, many of the 150 brokers trained rapidly lost interest, especially those with other more lucrative consulting opportunities (Maher, 1996).

The programme's limited impact holds lessons for intervention designed to influence business cooperation. The assumption behind the programme was that small firms would wish to join a network because it would be easier and less risky than entering export markets alone (Ffowcs Williams, 1996). By the sharing of resources and undertaking joint investments, small firms could compete as if they were a large firm while still retaining their own identities and core competencies. Optimistically, it was also noted that there was no constraint on the number of networks that might be joined. In practice, such possibilities need to be balanced against the motivations for being in business and the difficulty of maintaining agreement over inputs and returns from a venture on which individual participants are likely to have differing degrees of dependence. Getting small firms to cooperate is highly problematic wherever you are. Even in Denmark it has been observed that attempting to accelerate cooperation amongst businesses that have little prior familiarity with each other was likely to be fraught with "serious problems" (Henriksen, 1995).

Publicity material from New Zealand's hard network programme suggests that interest came mainly from small-scale producers or service providers seeing potential in adopting a common identity and sharing business publicity. Such horizontal networks bring together participants who have similar skills and resource needs. This form of network addresses marketing weaknesses and responds to the increased concentration of retail ownership. Indeed, several of the networks started prior to the network programme. Obtaining cooperation amongst firms operating in different parts of the value chain represents a more significant development than horizontal integration but is harder to establish. At the outset there may be few areas of common experience, different perspectives on the aspects of their business critical to performance or possibly a history of adversarial relationships with the businesses in their value chain. When projects are identified, implementation exposes networks to even greater challenges. Perhaps inevitably firms will have different dependencies on the network and different perceptions of the potential returns and barriers to 'going it alone'.

The evidence in Denmark was that once public subsidies were withdrawn, networks rapidly ceased to function (Huggins, 1996; Amphion Report cited in Akoorie, 1998). Even with the much greater investment in the programme in Denmark, where networks received an average public subsidy of over US$250,000 (Henriksen, 1995; OECD, 1995, p 90), its impact there was also negligible. Consequently, the limited impact of the scheme in New Zealand probably says little about the business environment and more about the need for public policy to be guided by realistic assessments of the scope to accelerate business cooperation.

Business Clusters

The third policy intervention involves the promotion of business clusters. These initiatives are linked to Trade New Zealand which at one stage had a programme of "cluster musters" designed to encourage local communities to identify and promote their pockets of business specialisation (Ffowcs Williams, 1997a). The idea for this approach was partly inspired by images of Silicon Valley and North Italy's craft industry communities, as well as being encouraged by the Porter Project investigation. That study had identified several specialised local economies, such as the fishing industry in Nelson, where particular opportunities for strengthening business competitiveness through cooperation were thought to exist. More recently, local government has taken the lead in the promotion of business clusters as well as being advocates of further government support for this work through the Economic Development Association of New Zealand. Amongst the clusters that have been identified for promotion are boat building and film production in Waitakere City; earthquake engineering, film and television and 'creative content' in Wellington; seafood, aviation and horticulture in Nelson; forestry in Rotorua; and electronics in Christchurch.

Enthusiasm for the potential of business clusters runs high amongst advocates, not only in New Zealand but also overseas. This interest reflects a real contradiction in the progress of economic globalisation. Modern communications and organisational capacities have greatly extended the location options for business, but actual location remains remarkably 'sticky'. In many industries a few places remain centres of particular specialisations and their attractiveness shows little inclination to weaken. The prime example of this is Silicon Valley, the original home of semi-conductor manufacture that, even after several technological twists has sustained its status as the premier cluster of the new information and communications industry. Clustering is a real phenomenon but there is difficulty transferring this experience, especially to a small economy where clusters cannot attain international significance. This section explains this perspective first by a comment on business cluster theory, followed by two contrasting contexts in which cluster promotion is being attempted in New Zealand:

(i)   specialised economies; and
(ii)   clusters of minority activities.

Cluster Theory

Business clusters are generally envisaged as "geographically bounded concentrations of interdependent businesses with active channels for business transactions, dialogue and communications, that collectively share common opportunities and threats" (see OECD, 1996). Such localities are suggested to obtain many advantages over non-specialised economies, including:

- The concentration of firms in a related set of activities enables the emergence of collective resources, such as labour skills, market information, training agencies and raw material suppliers as well as pulling in buyers.
- Proximity facilitates subcontracting and joint contracting ties between neighbours. This helps firms to specialise which, in turn, can reduce risk by enabling the resources of other firms to be drawn upon before adding to internal capacity.
- Firms in a cluster compete and the proximity amongst competitors can exert extra pressure to innovate in response to competition.

- Clusters help new firms start up. They give access to industry skills, a concentrated customer base, subcontracting opportunities and support agencies that are familiar with the industry.
- The locality may acquire a marketing reputation enabling individual firms to trade on a collective marketing identity rather than having to invest in their own marketing.

Silicon Valley in California, North Italy's many industrial districts and biotechnology in Boston are amongst the examples cited of the existence of cluster advantages and the potential for the diffusion of clusters. These claims need to be judged against two main issues:

1. There are no precise rules about when a cluster exists and consequently the phenomenon is easily exaggerated. For example, must companies in the cluster interact with each other? If so, what proportion of business must be within the cluster? Does it matter if the cluster comprises a few big firms, or are we only dealing with concentrations of small firms? As well, the scale of the cluster substantially affects its significance, but once again no guidance exists on the volume of business needed for a cluster. For example, Silicon Valley constitutes a larger economy than all of New Zealand. It is home to many of the world's most rapidly growing companies and has a global reputation for innovation that pulls in financial, entrepreneurial and labour resources. It is hard to see what parallels exist between this locality and a group of twenty or so small companies in Wellington or wherever they may be in New Zealand.

2. Cluster advocates suggest that twin processes are at work: an increase in industry participation, as new opportunities for small companies arise and large organisations fragment; plus the clustering of those participants. The geographical clustering of industry may also reflect increased ownership concentration and a reduction of industry participants. Where the latter occurs, clustering is typically associated with large ownership units whose attachment to and dependence on any particular locality is less than a small enterprise. Across the Nordic region, industries exhibiting increased agglomeration are almost three times more likely to involve industries with declining participation than increasing participation (Maskell et al, 1998, p 61). The number of industries experiencing reduced agglomeration actually exceeds

the number experiencing increased participation and spatial concentration.

The scope to capture the potential benefits of clusters has also to be considered. Most enthusiasts envisage clusters as localities with a high degree of inter-firm interaction, in which firms both compete with each other and collaborate when it is advantageous to combine resources. In New Zealand, rather than this equality of dependence and interaction, local economies are probably more likely to be dominated by a few major players with multiple locations and linkages. Organisations with a resource base extending beyond the immediate cluster will need unusual incentives to make particular commitments to any single cluster.

A Specialised Economy Cluster – Nelson and Seafood
The Porter Project investigation identified Nelson's cluster of seafood-linked activity as one of the few functioning clusters that had developed spontaneously. The emergence of Nelson as an important centre for the seafood industry was partly an outcome of the broader development of the New Zealand fishing industry. In a little over 30 years, the fishing industry developed from an insignificant coastal fishery into one of the top five export sectors based on deep sea, shellfish and crustacean production (Sharp, 1998). Nelson became an important centre for the new seafood industry because of its established in-shore fishery and its centrality to the new deep sea fishing grounds. Around 70% of the national fishing quota is held by companies with a base in Nelson (Ffowcs Williams, 1997b). The largest operator (Sealord) has its corporate headquarters in Nelson, and the co-partner in the third largest operation (Talleys) has its home base in nearby in Motueka, although both are national operations with on-shore processing capacity at various strategic locations.

Nelson and seafood represent a prospect for leveraging advantage from a business cluster. It has national prominence in the industry; location advantages; and accumulated expertise within its fishing companies and a range of supporting businesses involved in vessel repairs and maintenance, engineering, fabrication, processing technology and food research. The deep sea fishing that takes place from Nelson, which includes fishing at extreme depths, has produced capture and processing methods that are unique to New Zealand. This expertise is increasingly being sought by foreign fishery organisations. As well, support companies have developed new markets including, for example, the servicing of tuna vessels that fish in the southwest Pacific.

There is cooperation between fishing companies because of common concerns with the administration of the quota management system and through business operations (for example, through the sharing of vessels, trading of quota and use of common facilities around the port). Nelson has two research centres that respectively specialise in seafood harvest and processing technology, and a polytechnic providing various grades of training for the industry. Collective research initiatives have included the Challenger Scallop and Dredge Oyster Fishery Management Companies. The nearby Marlborough Sounds are the centre of a greenshell mussel industry, a New Zealand trademark product. In 1997, seafood directly provided 11.5% of the region's employment and, in the three years to 1997, the annual employment growth was almost 10%, or twice the national average (Frater et al, 1998).

A Nelson Seafood Industry Cluster Group was set up in 1991 to encourage businesses in the cluster to retain its advantages and collectively to pursue opportunities to strengthen it. The group no longer meets although it continues to have a coordinator, and former participants suggest that it would be activated if collective issues arose. Its past activity included the preparation of a map identifying seafood industry participants and, more substantially, dialogue with the School of Fisheries at Nelson Polytechnic with respect to training needs. That dialogue resulted in initiatives to encourage more positive attitudes towards the industry amongst school leavers.

Within the Nelson community there are differing views about the present status of the cluster. A chief executive of one of the larger fishing companies reflected one perspective:

> When the cluster proposal was announced, we were interested because a cluster exists and is an important aspect of being in Nelson. [Our] operations are totally dependent on local services and infrastructure ... without whom this would not be the deep sea fishing capital of the South Pacific. Within the cluster, relationships work well, there is mutual inter-dependence ... This has not just been a case of tendering out services but also building up preferred providers and working with them for mutual advantage with long-term contracts.

> At the same time, for [us] cooperation is essentially about national initiatives and relationships ... Geographical boundaries are not important to cooperation. We have seen some opportunities for strengthening the cluster ... [but we] have several location options where there is spare capacity and do not need extra capacity in Nelson.

> The cluster functions without being given a label. The cluster project has made no difference to the way [we] operate ... there is nothing the public sector can do to support the cluster ... it is a matter of good commercial relationships ...

Such perspectives, which are shared with other national businesses operating in the cluster, have brought different priorities to those of businesses entirely dependent on the cluster. An example is the congestion around the port. The near doubling of cargo volumes during the 1990s intensified competition for berthing space and stretched the capacity of bunkering and providoring services. Investment in new port facilities has eased some problems, but slipway capacity is no longer sufficient for the larger vessels operating in the deep sea fleet. Slipway expansion is generally viewed as vital to ensure the long-term future of the engineering services that support the deep sea fleet but, as alluded to in the quotation above, potential users do not share this priority. As well, in contrast to the growth of deep sea activity, the in-shore fishery has been struggling to survive. This has weakened industry training capacity as the in-shore industry was often a starting point for new entrants (Frater et al, 1998). Optimistic assessments of the potential for greenshell mussel sales and increased access to the coast for marine farms have shifted investment to competing aquaculture projects. If successful, this suggests prospects for the in-shore fishery are poor. As these developments show, there is much fragmentation in the cluster and little consensus over its development opportunities.

The larger community, by being presented as 'stakeholders' in the cluster, has had its expectations for dialogue with and access to businesses in the cluster increased. These expectations are problematic for the seafood companies. The sector has a poor image amongst many in the community, due to environmental concerns, the impacts of on-shore processing and a reputation for low status employment. The use of foreign crews and chartering of foreign vessels are further sources of resentment. Companies may understandably prefer a low profile in the community and not to promote Nelson's status as South Pacific's 'seafood capital'. In contrast, stakeholders have had their expectations raised about benefits that will accrue to them. They point out that there is no 'shopfront' for the industry such as a fish market or distinctive local seafood cuisine and no integration with tourism, organic foods or arts and crafts producers that are also an important part of the Nelson economy. A casual visitor, for example, is likely to remain ignorant of Nelson's importance as a seafood centre. Modern fishing methods and marketing do not generate the landscapes associated with traditional fishing ports, but 'stakeholders' accuse seafood companies of being unwilling to provide opportunities.

One of the few definite results of the cluster initiative has been the reorientation of courses taught at the Polytechnic School of Fisheries to better suit local industry needs. Recognition of the community as cluster stakeholders might improve dialogue and mutual understanding and unlock potential economic benefits from the image of being a 'seafood capital'. How significant such benefits can be is unclear, as is the extent to which industry-community dialogue can be achieved by the cluster alone.

Minority Clusters – Wellington's Cluster Projects

Wellington City Council has made cluster development a key project within its economic development strategy. It seeks to activate clusters by encouraging business managers from the targeted clusters to form steering groups that are provided administrative support and encouragement to maintain a programme of activities intended to knit the group together. From research and initial contact with possible cluster industries, it has been working with three groups since 1997: film and television, earthquake technology and creative content, which encompasses providers of content for information technology media (originally part of a larger IT cluster). The current status and challenges faced by these groups varies as does their responsiveness to the cluster initiative.

- Film and television is the most important in terms of employment and income. 'Wellywood' was estimated to generate about $379 million in 1999/2000 and directly generate over 3000 full-time equivalent jobs (Film Wellington, 1999). It is based around the region's long-established production facilities and one resident internationally known director, Peter Jackson, who is estimated to generate around a third of the cluster's earnings. Given the nature of film and television production, there is a tradition of working ties between different production specialisations and also a resistance to formalising the cluster grouping within the format being followed by the City Council. Its future depends on the ability to attract international production work, with its competitors including Auckland.

• Creative content has its origins in the work generated by Te Papa which provided high profile work for a mix of established and new design and information technology companies. The cluster project is seeking to retain this expertise in Wellington, partly by building on a collective reputation from Te Papa. Since the opening of the museum, the need to seek out new markets has provided a shared focus for the group. Some success can be claimed, including work obtained by several cluster members for a new war and peace discovery centre in France. The ongoing success of the cluster will be partly dependent on the extent to which Te Papa maintains international attention and opportunity for the continuous upgrading of skills amongst locally-based content providers.

• Earthquake engineering technology arises from the long-standing presence in Wellington of expertise relevant to the management of earthquake risks. This clustering was a product of Wellington's own earthquake risk and scientific interest in the university and a government research agency. The collective extent of this expertise has been known to the participants but without efforts to generate mutual advantage from this. The business participants are predominantly drawn from the local offices of international engineering consultancies. Cluster participants have formed an incorporated society with rules governing participation, producing a more formal membership structure than the other projects. Joint projects have so far included market investigations of overseas areas recently affected by earthquakes. It has yet to be established whether the collective expertise is going to generate new markets or how the group's dominance by multinational consultancy firms will affect exploitation of any emerging advantage.

These groupings are clearly still in formation, and it remains to be seen what priority participants will retain to the local cluster. Members of the earthquake engineering technology cluster were included in the survey of shared trust reported in the previous chapter. Their responses did not suggest any greater development of a cooperative culture than in the overall sample that indicates that significant barriers remain to be overcome. As well, the earthquake and creative content clusters rely mainly on contract work. The experience of the JAG programme was that large groups of contractors tend not to survive because of the competition between lead contractors and the tendency for subcontractors to align themselves to one or two main contractors. Across all clusters it remains to be established whether national or local coordination will be most useful.

Social Capital

'Social capital' refers to the features of social organisation, such as trust, norms and networks that can improve the efficiency of society by facilitating coordinated action (Putnam et al, 1993, p 167). The recent revival of interest in the role of social capital was originally directed at explaining the effectiveness of governmental institutions. It was observed in the case of Italy's provincial government that stronger institutions were created where the community had a tradition of participation in civic associations and other community groupings. This participation in local associations was interpreted as the source of the trust, motivation and support that distinguished the effectiveness of different provincial governments (Putnam et al, 1993). Similarly, social capital has become seen as an important agent in economic activity because of its capacity to foster high levels of trust and information sharing between economic agents.

There is much in common between the idea of social capital and shared trust. Both refer to the potential benefits arising from increased personal interaction on information sharing, reduced opportunistic behaviour and the willingness to coordinate resources in pursuit of common interests. These ideas have been gaining attention in New Zealand mainly from the perspective that a shortage of social capital may exist, as well as to recognise the importance of monitoring public policy for its impact on social capital (Robinson, 1997). That interest may seem at odds with the suggestion that shared trust ought to be an innate advantage of small industrial countries. In a small country, the degree of knowledge and familiarity amongst owners and managers is expected to be high because of the shared backgrounds and restricted number of players in the business community. A shared culture should mean that managers share many of the same beliefs, values and convictions that should help formal and informal interaction. In the case of New Zealand, the propensity for participation in group organisations is well established (Olssen, 1992). The survey reported in chapter 4 found that a majority of respondents believed that there was a high degree of personal familiarity, common background and shared culture amongst business owners and managers, and most agreed that this made cooperation relatively easy to establish. Similarly, the JAG experience seems to indicate that cooperation can be established quite quickly. Initial participants referred to the novelty of working with other businesses but subsequently most groups worked effectively, although necessarily this often reduced to small groups. The possibility that increased inequality, poverty, less 'family friendly' workplaces, extended work hours or other possible causes are eroding social capital are legitimate causes of concern. The evidence about the density and effectiveness of personal networks is sketchy and certainly there is a strong case for the importance of data collection to monitor the state of social capital (Spellerberg, 1997).

There is undoubtedly a risk of under-investment in social capital as the desired social relationships generate externalities that cannot be appropriated exclusively by those who facilitate its creation (World Bank, 1997, p 79). On the other hand, as an explanation for New Zealand's comparatively poor economic performance, attention may be better focused on the demand for social capital rather than its supply. The distinction between the supply and demand for social capital is not entirely clear as it is generally suggested that trust, the essential product of social capital, is created only through use. A separation can be envisaged if it is recognised that not all business systems stand to benefit from personal trust (as compared with reliance on the trust arising from mutual confidence in institutional and legal systems) and that business may vary in its perceived need for information and resource sharing.

In the case of the Nordic economies, it has been argued that shared trust has been of significance because of the existence of communal authority. The presence of communal authority makes shared trust significant to business through its impact on encouraging business specialisation and the associated willingness to support and participate in industry associations. In the case of New Zealand, it is suggested that communal authority is less well developed compared with the Nordic economies. This has been traced to differences in political histories and relationships with government. Without the impetus to engage in collective strategies, the suggestion is that rather than a shortage of social capital, a greater issue has been the absence of structures that may have capitalised on the existence of shared trust. In this context, it is suggested that facilitating environments in which shared trust can be exploited is a greater immediate priority than augmenting the creation of social capital.

Conclusion

The purpose of this chapter was to examine recent initiatives to promote business cooperation, to identify what they indicated about existing business relations and to determine priorities for future intervention. On both accounts most interest resides in the JAG programme, the initiative which has had most impact in encouraging business cooperation. At its peak, over 30 groups were active, usually involving participants with little or no previous experience of working collectively. Several have continued as encompassing and active groups beyond the termination of the programme, although this has been helped by some continuing support from Trade New Zealand. Others survive with reduced participation but with doubts over their long-term survival, as representatives suggest that without external support activity will be increasingly hard to sustain. Some of the JAGs were built upon existing industry associations, usually those supported by compulsory levies or corporate members. Otherwise they represented a novel departure compared with established industry associations in their focus on business development and the extent of member participation.

In contrast to the JAG legacy, the hard networks programme appears to have had little significant lasting impact. Whereas the JAG programme gave participants freedom to mould the structure of groups to their preferences, the hard networks programme prescribed a specific type of business alliance. The structure does not appear to have fitted business preferences, partly as the programme's assumptions about the ease of accelerating business cooperation were too simplistic. That experience indicates the importance of designing intervention to be of a form that intended users can adapt to their own priorities, subject to the general goal of promoting business cooperation. Cluster promotion is currently the focus of much expectation. The Nelson seafood cluster is indicative of some of the challenges that will be encountered in these projects. Businesses inevitably have mixed dependencies on their local economy and varying development capacities that make it hard to sustain cooperation within clusters and that raise doubts about the existence of benefits in clustering. Where cluster businesses are pursuing international markets, it has yet to be established that commitment to a local cluster will be a priority over participation in a national network. Going New Zealand-wide may provide stronger marketing advantages and a wider choice of business partners than reliance just on neighbours.

6 • Conclusion and Recommendations

The main purpose of this study has been to raise interest in considering what it means to be a small industrial country. The suggestion that New Zealand has something to learn from other small industrial countries is not entirely original. During 1999, government ministers visited Finland and Ireland to obtain industrial promotion ideas. A Treasury research paper indicated further the government interest in Finland (Frame, 2000). Care must be exercised before attempting to 'cherry pick' policy experiences. What works in one place will not necessarily work in another. Small industrial countries share similar development challenges and opportunities arising from the need to operate with open borders and to manage the economic and social vulnerabilities this gives rise to. This similarity justifies comparison of public policy experiences, but account needs to be taken of the legacies of contrasting institutional histories. This is particularly so in the comparison between New Zealand and the Nordic economies. Equally, it is this strong contrast that provides the opportunity for learning from each other.

Small Country Characteristics
The general experience of small industrial economies has made the case for maintaining open borders, mainly because of the need for specialisation and overseas markets to attain a competitive scale of production. Openness, it should be emphasised, has been assessed through trade statistics rather than the extent and impact of regulation. Nordic countries have in the past combined their trade openness with forms of regulation that were intended to protect individual industries, although sometimes with unintended consequences. The success of the Swedish furniture company Ikea, for example, can be accounted for partly by a bilateral agreement between suppliers and retailers of furniture that restricted entry to new competitors. As an outsider, Ikea was forced to find innovative ways of obtaining and distributing its furniture that eventually paid off in its now highly successful business formula. A contemporary example of Nordic regulation is Denmark's ban on the sale of canned drinks and the

requirement that drink suppliers must collect glass containers for recycling. This regulation has an environmental motivation but has also helped its national supplier, Carlsberg, to retain a near monopoly on domestic beer sales. The need for export markets requires that small countries minimise impediments to international trade but this does not necessarily mean the abandonment of all efforts to support industrial development.

The retention of a specialisation in low and medium technology activities is a second characteristic of small industrial countries. The high costs of building and retaining a presence in high technology industries has constrained small industrial country participation in activity that relies on large R&D budgets. There is variation between small countries in their technological dependencies. Nordic success in telecommunications is well known and Ireland has become a centre for information technology. For reasons explained in chapter 2, neither of these cases contradicts the main proposition that small countries must specialise in low to medium technology industries. For New Zealand, the implications are nonetheless unclear as the high technology share of employment and exports is low even amongst small countries. Some justification for addressing the under-representation exists, but the broader experience of small countries indicates that it is unrealistic to promote participation in high technology activities as an important part of an industrial development strategy.

A proclivity toward corporatist economic management has been proposed as a third small country characteristic. This claim has been rejected but it has drawn attention to the broader issue of how best to manage the vulnerability arising from the openness and exposure to the international economy. Nordic economies and New Zealand both recognised a need to cushion the impact on citizens of periodic economic dislocation, which has been the inevitable fate of small, specialised economies. The form in which this cushion has been provided has varied. The Nordic approach has traditionally stressed a willingness to accommodate economic change by compensating those affected by it through welfare and employment policies. The New Zealand approach has traditionally sought to restrain the impact of change by protecting existing employment and by maintaining a large sheltered sector of the economy. Neither approach was ultimately sustainable in terms of ensuring sufficient job creation in the competitive sector, although it has been argued that the Nordic arrangement of openness with compensation was less damaging to productivity in the competitive sector than New Zealand's protectionism.

As well, the Nordic approach had the further advantage of social modernisation by bringing into employment sections of society that benefited from the active labour market policies and expansion of public services.

Shared trust is a fourth attribute claimed to distinguish small industrial countries. Shared trust draws attention to the potential transparency of small country business communities. This arises from the comparatively unified culture amongst participants and the density of personal contact networks. Those attributes would seem to be uncontroversial. The Nordic claim that the transparency inevitably becomes a source of industrial strength is open to doubt. One reason for doubt is the absence of strong evidence of its significance in Nordic economies. A second doubt about the Nordic interpretation of shared trust is the need to consider contingent influences that might determine the extent of shared trust obtained in a small country.

It has been argued that communal authority has made the Nordic business system more open to cooperation than is the case in New Zealand. This argument is speculative as there are no comparative data to measure the state of communal authority, a concept which some people might seek to dismiss. In the absence of such empirical evidence, the claim has been supported by reference to:

(i)   the greater emphasis on strong welfare systems designed to retain national cohesion in the Nordic economies;
(ii)   the Nordic adherence to 'low voltage' politics and the emphasis on negotiation between interest groups compared with the tradition of adversarial politics and state-imposed solutions in New Zealand; and
(iii) business systems theory and its association between communal authority and known features of the Nordic economies, such as the status of industry associations and the accommodation of trade union influence.

If these arguments are correct, it would provide one reason why shared trust may be of greater significance in Nordic business systems than it appears to be in New Zealand. Communal authority is expected to encourage specialisation and the willingness to support collective organisations. These characteristics are propitious for shared trust. Specialisation promotes interest in business cooperation within industries.

Membership of industry associations provides opportunity for formal and informal interaction amongst business mangers.

Policy Implications

Various forms of corporatism have provided the context for business development in the Nordic economies but it is unrealistic to propose their replication in New Zealand. This possibility has previously been evaluated and rejected (Boston, 1986) when corporatism was a more viable development model than it is today (Pekkarinen, 1992). That judgement was based on an assessment, which proved correct, that corporatist accord was difficult to sustain in the context of diverging labour market trends. As well, the scale of the organisational, political and attitudinal changes that would be required to implant corporatist structures in New Zealand was considered to be too great. Since that judgement was made, the introduction of proportional representation has been a significant innovation that in the 1980s was perhaps thought unlikely to come about. On the other hand, the weakening of trade union influence and organisational capacity as a consequence of the Employment Contracts Act 1991 has counteracted that possible stimulus.

Proportional voting could be a step in the direction of corporatism if one political party emerges as an enduring core of successive coalition governments and that party aligns itself to one interest grouping. This would be a change from the context where the main parties have had a 'natural' support base but have remained comparatively open to all lobby groups. In the event that alignments became more rigid than in the past, either labour or employer interest groups (depending on whether Labour or National becomes the dominant party) might be inclined to pursue a degree of self-regulation with their opposite interest group in lieu of their lost political influence. Of course, for this to happen both interest groups would need to compromise. The re-introduction of a legal status for trade unions together with some rights of organisation under the Employment Relations Act 2000 has made that scenario slightly more plausible than it was in the 1990s but still unlikely. It remains uncertain how far trade union influence will spread in the context of labour market changes and business employment strategies that have weakened the coverage of collective employment contracts. A revival of trade union influence is likely to be accompanied by a diversity of union structures (industry, skill and enterprise-based) that will encourage different organisational priorities.

At the time the Employment Relations Act was passed, 83 trade unions existed representing 17.7% of the workforce compared with a similar number representing 41.5% of the workforce when the Employment Contracts Act 1991 was enacted. Corporatist arrangements require that a small number of encompassing unions represent the bulk of the workforce. As well, of course, there is still no sign that New Zealand will follow the pattern of other proportional voting systems and produce an enduring party of government.

For similar reasons that corporatism is not advocated, the possibility of a shift toward alliance ownership and changes in the relationships between business and finance are not considered. Neither the now largely foreign-owned finance industry nor existing business owners are likely to entertain such a reorientation. Interest does exist in the strengthening of New Zealand-owned financial institutions, but this is motivated by concern over the access to services, primarily for low income and rural communities, and issues of national control rather than the promotion of alliance capitalism.

On the other hand, the relationships between communal authority, national cohesion and economic strength suggested by the Nordic experience deserve attention. As discussed in earlier chapters, the compensation policies of Nordic economies did not facilitate the degree of economic adjustment that some admirers claimed but it did bring other benefits. The perceived need for national cohesion continues to give broad acceptance of the need for strong welfare and labour market support. Business system theory links this emphasis on national cohesion to business behaviour that fits the potential strength of a small industrial country. National cohesion maintains communal authority and communal authority encourages business specialisation and cooperation. The links between welfare support, national cohesion, communal authority and industrial success – whilst intuitively appealing – have yet to be conclusively demonstrated. It is an area that invites investigation, particularly with regard to the attachment of business to their industry. Business system theory proposes that communal authority ties businesses into their respective sector specialisations. Out of this develops interest in business cooperation and support to industry associations to offset the risks of specialisation. These connections require examination in the New Zealand context.

The Nordic and New Zealand economies have experienced a revival of employment growth in the 1990s, but with the Nordic economies continuing to be more successful in combining employment growth with increasing and high income per capita. This at least suggests that combining open markets with some forms of compensation for adjustment can be a successful strategy. The New Zealand attempt to combine free trade with deregulated labour markets and minimal welfare has not matched those achievements. Inherited marketing advantages and industrial strengths contribute to the performance difference but caution in the liberalisation route would also seem to be indicated.

Despite uncertainties over the role of shared trust in the Nordic economies, there are several reasons to propose that public policy should give attention to its status in New Zealand. First, shared trust draws attention to the likelihood of personal familiarity within a small business community. This might be a source of strength but perhaps equally has the risk of accentuating conflicts amongst competitors. In this context, it would seem important to understand the nature of business relations in one's own community and to seek to foster relations that are most supportive of industry development. Second, there are reasons to believe that New Zealand is not capturing the benefits of shared trust and that the legacy of past institutional structures continues to be unconducive to business cooperation. Third, where the benefits of shared trust can be captured, it should bring two sources of business advantage:

(i)   discouragement to malfeasance, to the extent that mavericks who deviate from the 'rules of the game' in a small business community are identifiable and susceptible to collective sanctions; and

(ii) business cooperation should be stimulated because of the low barriers to entering and exiting relationships in the context of a common understanding of accepted business practices and obligations.

Business interaction and shared learning are potentially of particular significance to small industrial countries because of their specialisation in low-to-medium technology industries. This context gives opportunity to accumulate expertise and to gain the benefits of pooling knowledge.

Industry as the Arena for Change
Attempts to foster business cooperation in New Zealand have varied in the extent to which they have been nationally or locally based and whether

they have sought to encourage widespread or selective participation. A number of reasons suggest that industry is the most appropriate level of intervention. Industries comprise collections of individual enterprises and parts of enterprises that are united by their interest in a particular range of products and services and by their use of common technologies. These characteristics shape the structure of industries in terms of the number and size range of participants. Members of the industry compete with each other on terms that reflect the rivalry amongst existing operations, the extent of external threat (from new entrants or substitute products and services) and the bargaining power of suppliers and buyers. The balance of forces promoting rivalry and common threats gives each industry its distinct culture and varying opportunities for collective learning and resource sharing. The extent and form of business cooperation will differ between industries and this needs to be accommodated in any intervention to encourage cooperation.

An alternative to an industry approach is to foster cooperation within business clusters. Advocacy of this method is justified by reference to well-known examples of successful clusters and the assumption that these cases reflect a trend toward location specialisation. There is little evidence to support the claims of a business preference for clustering, as shown in the Nordic data referred to in chapter 5. Moreover, New Zealand lacks the conditions that have promoted business clusters in a country such as Italy, which is a precedent for clusters commonly cited by advocates, such as strong regional differences, traditions of artisan business and the pooling of contracts in 'putting out' systems of work. In contrast, New Zealand is populated by national and increasingly international scales of enterprise that have varying attachments to the localities in which they operate. This is not to deny entirely the value of public support to fledgling clusters of new enterprise, such as those in Wellington. It does suggest that the outcomes will be modest because successful members of the cluster will make their own linkages as their business grows. In the case of established activities, as was referred to in the case of Nelson, it is mainly around national resources and issues that businesses are motivated to participate in collective projects. This brings us back to the industry as the key arena for building business cooperation.

An Agenda for Industry Associations
Accepting a focus on industry as the arena in which to encourage business

cooperation, priority to the strengthening of industry associations can be justified on several grounds:

- Effective industry associations provide one mechanism for strengthening shared trust. Industry associations can promote cooperation by providing opportunities for formal and informal interaction, including participation in collective industry projects, as well as by raising the costs to being an 'outsider' where membership of the association confers significant benefits. Moreover, the need to strengthen business cooperation in New Zealand has been recognised by others as an important aspect of contemporary 'best practice' (Crocombe at al, 1991; Knuckey et al, 1999).

- Trade New Zealand's promotion of JAGs provides existing public policy experience to draw on in both justifying and designing further support to industry associations.

- Industry groups are already being called upon to assist in the delivery of public policy goals, including training and guidance on the allocation of public R&D expenditure. Consequently, as well as any benefits for shared trust, strengthening industry associations can have spill-over benefits to other policy areas if industry associations become effective channels for public policy.

- It is generally accepted that industry associations have been weak and fragmented and concerned more with managing existing situations than business development. The main exceptions to this are groups that benefit from compulsory levies, a corporate membership or Trade Development Board assistance. The New Zealand Business Roundtable has been viewed as an exception in its effectiveness and participation from its constituency (Wanna, 1989; Roper, 1993). Having commenced in the mid-1970s as an informal grouping of leading industrialists, it became an organised and well-resourced lobby group in pursuit of its free market agenda (Deeks et al, 1994). During the 1990s, the Roundtable lost membership and had less impact when its focus shifted from trade and labour market regulation to the dismantling of rural sector producer boards, suggesting that even it was challenged by organisational weaknesses (Cronin, 1997).

- Obtaining membership is harder generally for industry associations than it is for labour organisations (Wanna, 1989). Individual business organisations have less need to rely on a collective organisation to gain access to key decision-makers than do employees. Incentives to encourage participation are therefore often accepted as necessary where the target is to build encompassing associations that have significant resources and some capacity to manage collective strategies.

• Beyond the strategic significance of associations, their role as suppliers of individual services can bring benefits to members over the use of independent service vendors. Associations benefit from their relationship to members, access to unique industry knowledge, the capacity to maintain highly specific assets (including staff expertise and industry data from membership surveys), the interconnectedness of many transactions and their complexity (as when dealing with government).

Of course, policy intervention can create its own problems especially where this extends to compulsory membership. Compulsion cannot ensure commitment, and it may be perceived as too restrictive on enterprise and become an additional source of resistance. Alternative ways of influencing the willingness to join associations include financial incentives, either to projects with eligibility dependent on membership of a qualifying association or to the ongoing work of its executive, or the selective 'recognition' of associations. With the latter approach, associations with preferred characteristics, such as a representative membership and authority delegation, are given rights of participation denied to individual businesses. A further and least directive approach is through competitions, awards and challenges to recognise the achievements of existing associations so as to raise their status and to encourage membership and replication in other industries.

Even with the wide range of policy options, it is worth recognising that differences often exist between what government would like an association to deliver and the priority of an association to meet its members' needs. Broadly there are two types of demand that can give rise to a business association, although the separation can at times be blurred (Grant, 1993):

1. Collective influence: this may involve the setting of industry standards, codes of conduct, quality standard branding, collective representation to government and the collection of data on industry performance trends. Such collective services are typically funded by

general membership subscriptions rather than fee-for-service payments.

2. Customised services: this involves the provision of services purchased by individual members and paid for separately from the membership fee.

For government, an association is a viable channel for information exchange and policy delivery when it represents the collective voice of a broad constituency and when it can maintain adherence to shared strategies (Bennett, 1997). For associations, a focus on collective influence is likely to capture a low proportion of the total potential membership as collective services have externality benefits for both joiners and non-joiners ('free riders'). A small group reduces the risk of advantages being captured by non-joiners, and for this reason may be preferred by members, but it reduces the association's collective influence and can accentuate its resource constraints. The addition of service functions can act to undermine the ability of the association to offer collective representation because of the resistance to paying both fees for services and a large subscription fee. Where membership is voluntary, a tension can then arise between what governments would like associations to deliver and what associations can most readily supply (Bennett, 1997, p 9).

The extent of tension between government and member priorities depends partly on the ability to recruit members. The degree of competition between firms in itself may not be a barrier to the formation of an association (Grant, 1993). Firms that are vigorous competitors can still find common issues to deal with, such as relations with government, access to international markets or labour relations. Associations typically establish rules to ensure that sensitive commercial data are kept confidential, such as the use of external parties rather than executive staff to collect data from members. More critical to 'collective associability' than competitiveness is the heterogeneity of members.

An association with a single type of member (for example, all small firms or all large firms) is generally easier to manage than a mixed membership. Typically a few firms tend to assume a disproportionate role in any association, providing the members of the executive, committees and any project teams. In a mixed member association, it is likely to be large firms that make this contribution. This can have advantages in increasing the resources and leadership available to the association. It can also result in resentment and disinterest in the association amongst members from small organisations where they feel that their interests are not being adequately represented. Similarly, business specialisation that increases dependence on an individual sector is expected to increase participation as specialised businesses have a greater incentive to manage risk through collective strategies with other members of their industry than do multi-activity organisations. A feature of German business associations, for example, has been the apportionment of market and technology specialisations amongst individual members (Herrigel, 1989; Sabel, 1994).

In practice it can be hard to observe the influence of membership characteristics because associations can be unresponsive to changes in their industry. A strong tendency to 'path dependency' has been observed with associations in which many "exist because they existed in the past, associations tend to wither rather than to die" (Bennett, 1997, p 8). Typically, associations do not easily come into existence. The uncertainties associated with the calculation of costs and benefits as well as the possibility of capturing benefits without joining induce caution in taking up membership. Inertia encourages the retention of the original structure and focus especially, it has been suggested, where members rather than a professional executive manage the association. As a result, associations in voluntary systems tend to survive with a relatively stable membership and range of activities, perhaps without ever fulfilling their full potential as judged by either outsiders or insiders. This kind of situation was described in a survey of New Zealand industry associations completed in the early 1990s (Enderwick and Wilson, 1992). The researchers found little evidence of adaption to the need for business to generate new sources of competitiveness, characterising them as poorly positioned for dealing with change, reactive and bastions of the status quo. In this context, it was largely through the efforts of Trade New Zealand that associations started to play a proactive business development role.

Five Suggestions

First, there is a need to obtain understanding of the present status of industry associations. Surveys up to the early 1990s confirm their weakness and fragmentation. Following the Employment Contracts Act 1991, many employer unions have ceased to exist (Deeks et al, 1994), but the impact of the new competitive environment on trade associations remains unclear.

In sectors such as forestry and seafood, the presence of large corporates has resulted in new representative structures consistent with the preference of corporates for reduced government influence in their sector. Amongst small-firm dominated sectors, groups such as the Automotive Parts and Accessories Association continue to operate in the face of the closure of the car assembly industry that may be indicative of the tenacity of trade associations to survive. Some new roles and opportunities for trade associations have arisen with the establishment of industry training organisations and the encouragement from Trade New Zealand, although this tended to result in new groups rather than the strengthening of existing ones. For associations linked to the primary sector, the ability to collect compulsory levies has sustained well-resourced associations that can play important roles in business development, such as the Wine Institute of New Zealand. In other cases, such as export flowers, the potential introduction of compulsory levies is the subject of intense debate over their justification. The overall level of satisfaction business managers have with their opportunities to participate in collective organisations, as well as the level of support they give, are unknown. Neither is it known what if any role associations play in encouraging shared trust or 'hard' forms of business cooperation. Previous studies, referred to above and in earlier chapters, have stressed the fragmented and poorly resourced condition of resources as evidence of their limited capacity to promote business competitiveness. This judgement needs to be updated.

Second, 'sector challenges' should be organised by a government agency to reward industry associations that are judged to develop the most effective programmes to support their sector's development. Such an approach is already partly undertaken with the annual export awards that include a "cooperating to compete" category, most recently awarded to one of the former JAGs, the Marine Export Group (Marex). The Foresight Project organised by the Ministry of Research, Science and Technology has been a further precedent for the setting of sector challenges. This challenge was to produce a vision of the sector's future preferred development and to identify the science and technology needs to achieve that vision (Ministry of Research, Science and Technology, 1998). It resulted in around 140 responses, predominantly from a mix of social, health, Maori, environmental and locality groups, but industry also participated. The responses from industry groups varied in meeting the Foresight expectations, and generally the comparatively well-resourced primary sector groups were considered more rigorous than those from manufacturing or service industries. The willingness to take up a challenge and the quality of outputs can be enhanced by administrative support to groups that join the programme. That support can be provided as an incentive to participate as well as the usefulness of the end product being an encouragement to take up the challenge. The scope of the challenges set needs to be consistent with the delivery capacity. In this context, long-term strategies such as Foresight might be of less value than challenges that recognise immediate achievements associated with obtaining and assisting their membership. At present most associations have limited influence to ensure compliance to long-term strategies, nor do they necessarily have members with a dedicated industry commitment.

Third, the identification and promotion of a 'model industry association' would provide opportunity for groups to benchmark their own group against an ideal. Such a model would appropriately cover the services provided by the group, its governance and its level of representation. The delineation of model attributes clearly needs to be grounded in what is currently realistic, and what can be achieved without the resources provided by compulsory levies or participation from wealthy corporate groups (although some attention to the specific activities of such 'privileged' groups is appropriate).

There are a number of groups, particularly amongst those former JAGs that have built themselves into encompassing and largely self-sustaining groups, that provide possible sources for a model within the reach of 'normal' industries. This includes Marex, the Pine Manufacturers Association and the Organic Producers Export Network, each of which provides valued business support to groups of mainly small and medium-sized companies. The case of the Organics group is particularly impressive for its success in sustaining cooperation between 100% organic producers and mixed organic/conventional producers. The Pine Manufacturers Association has evolved from a focus on market education initiatives to business development support, with the target of assisting manufactured timber products to increase their share of timber exports from 10% to 30%. Another interesting aspect of this group is a 'buddy' system in which a member on the executive is responsible for reporting to two to four other members, as a supplement to e-mail circulation of meeting reports. To support the diffusion of model practices, it may be appropriate for a public agency to support assistance for groups to undertake benchmarking, as either one-off exercises or through the mechanism of a 'benchmarking club'.

Four, as mentioned in chapter 5, before the winding up of the JAG programme, Trade New Zealand had considered the possibility of amalgamating individual JAGs into three broad sector-based associations. This would have produced economies in administration while maintaining a forum through which participation in their new export networks scheme could have been promoted. Support for this approach was mixed amongst the JAGs but it was generally considered a useful initiative by the coordinators of those former JAGs that have made some effort to remain as a group, although typically these groups are now less active than they were. Trade New Zealand's abandonment of the 'mega-JAG' structure reflected the constraints on its funding (both the total budget and its need to focus exclusively on export promotion) and its concern to widen participation in export networks compared with their previous distribution of export assistance. From a broader business development perspective, acknowledging that the benefits to JAG members were always gained in domestic and export markets (Perry, 1995), there is reason to revive the mega-JAG proposal. It would provide a way of retaining the expertise and trust accumulated within the JAGs and contribute to the generation of new projects that might be implemented through the export networks scheme.

Five, the objective should be set of establishing a systematic relationship between government and industry associations in which productive two-way communication is maintained over issues affecting business development. The present pattern is one of 'government push' periodically to demand inputs from associations that are often inadequately resourced or established to provide meaningful responses. The ideal would be to work towards a position where there is 'customer pull' as well, reflected in the capacity for industry associations to originate proposals to government for business development partnerships. In the past, for example, the Manufacturers' Association has been critical of Trade New Zealand sponsorship of industry groups without itself being in a position fully to develop its own proposals for how this support might be devolved or having the capacity to participate in the programme's administration. This environment can produce a perception that government agencies are usurping the role that associations try to perform. Unless this perception is corrected and opportunities for partnership are strengthened, the frequent setting of challenges is likely to bring diminishing returns.

Concluding Summary

It has become popular to claim that the nation state is of declining significance. In a world of instant telecommunications, global corporations and unifying consumer cultures it has been fashionable to claim that we now live in a borderless world. Compared with this vision of seamless territories, this investigation into small industrial economies has been distinctly old fashioned. It has stressed the relevance of inherited institutions, politics and social relations and suggested that their influence is not simply erased by deregulating markets and removing investment controls. This has been illustrated through the comparison with the Nordic economies which has drawn attention to differences in the incorporation of interest groups into decision-making, welfare policy and trade openness. Broadly, while the Nordic economies have emphasised the sharing of political control between government and interest groups, strong welfare systems and open borders, New Zealand has had strong governments and weak interest groups, residual welfare systems and, at least until recently, trade protection. The source of this difference is partly in New Zealand's modern development as a settler society in which all sections of the community looked to the state for security and the development of necessary public services. In the Nordic region, employers and labour groups in the export sector had reasons to favour self-regulation and cooperation between themselves rather than relying on the state to manage economic relationships to the degree that happened in New Zealand.

The industrial conciliation and arbitration (IC&A) system was of particular importance to New Zealand's business system. It effectively took away the need for strong, participative employer associations. Although now long abandoned, this inherited institutional culture provides one possible explanation for the continuing weakness and fragmentation of industry groups. In turn, commitment to an industry is a starting point for business cooperation. Where the fate of a business is locked into a particular sector, other things being equal, the incentive to cooperate with other industry participants is expected to be high.

The post-1984 dismantling of trade protection has brought New Zealand closer to the small industry country norm. Differences remain with respect to the conditions that can encourage business cooperation. The opportunity for a small business community to build competitiveness, from the advantages of its comparative cultural homogeneity and density of personal contact networks, appears to be unrealised in the case of New

Zealand. It is not an original message that business in New Zealand should give more consideration to cooperation than it has. The Porter Project report and Trade New Zealand have both echoed this recommendation. The Nordic-New Zealand comparison adds to the case for cooperation by:

(i)   identifying the origins of structural differences in business organisation that help to explain the relative absence of cooperation in New Zealand;
(ii) emphasising the impediments to high tech industries and stressing the need to focus on development within medium and low tech sectors; and
(iii) providing evidence of the significance of cooperation in sustaining international competitiveness.

There is some evidence from the recent Ministry of Commerce best practice survey (Knuckey et al, 1999) that attitudes may be changing, but that has not been confirmed from the assessment of shared trust. The need to encourage business cooperation would appear to remain.

Effective industry associations provide one starting point for strengthening shared trust. Industry associations can promote cooperation by providing opportunities for formal and informal interaction, including participation in collective industry projects, as well as by raising the costs to being an 'outsider' where membership of the association confers significant benefits. It is generally accepted that New Zealand's industry associations have been weak and fragmented and concerned more with managing existing situations than with promoting business development. This is partly understandable as obtaining membership is harder for industry associations than generally it is for labour organisations. Individual business organisations have less need to rely on a collective organisation to gain access to key decision-makers than do employees. Active industry associations can be found, but mainly where they have the benefit of compulsory levies (for example, the Wine Institute of New Zealand), a corporate membership (the Business Roundtable) or Trade Development Board support (such as the Pine Manufacturing Association, the Organic Producers Export Network and the Marine Export Group). As with these examples, either compulsion or strong incentives are needed to encourage participation, especially where the target is to build encompassing associations that have significant resources and some capacity to manage collective strategies. The incentive to join industry groups can be assisted by government. Financial support may enhance the services provided by associations. As well, competitions, awards and challenges can recognise the achievements of existing associations so as to raise their status and to encourage membership and replication in other industries. Whatever the methods to be employed, Nordic experience points to the urgency of strengthening the capacity for collective action and shared learning within the New Zealand business community.

Appendix • List of Interviewees

1. Industry Groups

Jon Manhire and Samira Wohlfart, Organic Products Exporters Group
Marcia Dunnett and Rex Baynes, New Zealand Manufacturers' Federation Inc
Jim Boys, Aviation Training and Education New Zealand
John Valentine, The New Zealand Seafood Industry Council Ltd
Andrew Branson, Hoki Fishery Management Co Ltd
Leicester Chatfield, Cosmex of New Zealand
Tony Phillips and Vicki Vachias, New Zealand Furniture
David Easton, New Zealand Flower Exporters Association
Lane Finley, New Zealand Marine Export Group
Owen Embling, New Zealand Plastic Exporters Group
Anne-Marie McKenzie, Wine Institute of New Zealand
David Withy, Constructive Solutions
James Griffiths, New Zealand Forest Industries Council
Lawrie Halkett, New Zealand Pine Manufacturers Association
Michael-John Loza and Collier Isaacs, New Zealand Game Industry Board
Tanya Reid, FoodSystems of New Zealand
Evan Morch, Defence Technologies
Murray Chapman, Homes New Zealand

2. Government Agencies

Stephen Knuckey, Ministry of Commerce
Paul Gandar and Pam Mazoyer, Ministry of Research, Science & Technology
Steve Wilcox, Waitakere City Council
Shanne Morrissey, Capital Development Agency, Wellington City Council
Richard Butler, Nelson City Council
Tim Harris, Alan Norton and Mike Hannah, New Zealand Trade Development Board

117

3. Other

Michèle Akoorie, Marketing and International Management, University
    of Waikato
Colin Campbell-Hunt, School of Business & Public Management, Victoria
    University of Wellington
Graeme Robertson, Cawthron Institute
Charles Hufflett, Solander Group

References

Akoorie, M (1998) 'Encouraging small firm internationalisation: a tripartite examination of recent policy prescriptions in Denmark, Australia and New Zealand', Hamilton: Department of Marketing and International Management, University of Waikato

Amin, A and D Thomas (1996)'The negotiated economy: state and civic institutions in Denmark', *Economy and Society* 25 (2): 255-81

Amstrup, N (1976) 'The perennial problem of small states: a survey of research efforts', *Cooperation and Conflict* 11: 163-82

Australian Manufacturing Council/Manufacturers Advisory Group (AMC/MAG) (1994) *Leading the Way: A Study of Best Manufacturing Practice in Australia and New Zealand*, Wellington: Ministry of Commerce

Bassett, M (1979) *Getting Together Again*, Henderson: P J Harris

Bennett, R (1997) 'The relation between government and business associations in Britain: an evaluation of recent developments', *Policy Studies* 18 (1): 5-33

Berrefjord, O and P Heum (1993) 'Non-market governance of business in a market-based economy: the case of Norway', in S-E Sjostrand (ed.) *Institutional Change, Theory and Empirical Findings*, New York: M E Sharpe

Boston, J (1986) 'Is corporatism a viable model for New Zealand', *New Zealand Journal of Business* 8: 1-13

Bray, M and M Perry (1994) 'Public sector science, innovation and the market: lessons from the DSIR', *New Zealand Journal of Science* 51 (2): 45-50

Britton S, R Le Heron and E Pawson (1993) *Changing Places in New Zealand: A Geography of Restructuring*, Christchurch: New Zealand Geographic Society

Brooking, T (1992) 'Economic transformation', in G Rice (ed.) *The Oxford History of New Zealand*, Auckland: Oxford University Press

Brosnan P, P Walsh and P Rowe (1985) 'Democracy and decision making in unions of employers', *New Zealand Journal of Business* 7: 1-12

Cartwright, W (1993) 'Multiple linked 'diamonds' and the international competitiveness of export-dependent industries: the New Zealand experience', *Management International Review* 33 (2): 55-70

Castles, F (1985) *The Working Class and Welfare*, Sydney: George Allen & Unwin

Castles, F (1988) *Australia Public Policy and Economic Vulnerability*, Sydney: Allen & Unwin

Castles, F (1989) 'Social protection by other means Australia's strategy of coping with external vulnerability', in F Castles (ed.) *The Comparative History of Public Policy*, Cambridge: Polity Press

Chase-Dunn, C (1989) *Global Formation: Structures of the World Economy*, Oxford: Basil Blackwell

Christiansen, P (1994) 'A negotiated economy? Public regulation of the manufacturing sector in Denmark', *Scandinavian Political Studies* 17 (4): 305-19

Coe, N (1997) 'US transnationals and the Irish software industry: assessing the nature, quality and stability of a new wave of foreign direct investment', *European Urban and Regional Studies* 4 (3): 211-230

Cookson, C (1998) 'The R&D scoreboard', *Financial Times*, 25 June

Corbett, L (1990) *Manufacturing Strategies: The 1990 New Zealand Manufacturing Futures Survey*, Wellington: Graduate School of Business and Government Management, Victoria University of Wellington

Corbett, L (1992) *Turning Point in Manufacturing: the 1992 New Zealand Manufacturing Futures Survey*, Wellington: Graduate School of Business and Government Management, Victoria University of Wellington

Corbett, L (1996) *New Zealand Manufacturing: Strategies and Performance 1996, Summary Report of the 1996 New Zealand Manufacturing Futures Survey*, Special Report Series 9, Wellington: Graduate School of Business and Government Management, Victoria University of Wellington

Corbett, L (1998) *New Zealand Manufacturing: Strategies and Performance 1996, Summary Report of the 1996 New Zealand Manufacturing Futures Survey*, Wellington: Graduate School of Business and Government Management, Victoria University of Wellington

Crocombe G, M Enright and M Porter (1991) *Upgrading New Zealand's Competitive Advantage*, Auckland: Oxford University Press

Cronin, B (1997) 'The decline of the Business Roundtable', paper presented at the New Zealand Political Studies Association conference, Hamilton: Waikato University, 8 June

Curtis, B (1993) 'The export meat industry', in *Labour, Employment and Work in New Zealand*, Proceedings of the Fifth Conference, Wellington: Victoria University of Wellington, 12-13 November

Dalum B, U Jorgensen and J Fagerberg (1988) 'Small open economies in the world market for electronics: the case of the Nordic countries', in C Freeman and B-A Lundvall (eds) *Small Countries Facing the Technological Revolution*, London: Pinter Publishers

Dalum, B and G Villumsen (1996) *Are OECD Export Specialisations 'Sticky'? Relations to the Convergence-Divergence Debate*, Working Paper 96-3, Aalborg: Danish Research Unit for Industrial Dynamics, Aalborg University

Dalziel, P (1989) 'The economic summit: what people were thinking', in B Easton (ed.) *The Making of Rogernomics*, Auckland: Auckland University Press

Deeks J, J Parker and R Ryan (1994) *Labour and Employment Relations in New Zealand*, Second edition, Auckland: Longman Paul

Danish Technological Institute (DTI) (1994) 'First assessment and recommendations on a business network programme in New Zealand', Unpublished report prepared by the Danish Technological Institute for the New Zealand Trade Development Board, Wellington

Edquist, C and B-A Lundvell (1993) 'Comparing the Danish and Swedish systems of innovation', in R Nelson (ed.) *National Innovation Systems*, New York: Oxford University Press

Enderwick, P and L Wilson (1992) 'Improving New Zealand's international competitiveness: the contributions of industry associations', *New Zealand Journal of Business* 14: 26-49

Fagerberg, J (1995) 'User producer interaction, learning and comparative advantage, *Cambridge Journal of Economics* 19 (1): 243-56

Ffowcs Williams, I (1996) 'New Zealand: The internationalisation of competition and the emergence of networks', in *Networks of Enterprises and Local Development*, Paris: Organisation for Economic Cooperation and Development

Ffowcs Williams, I (1997a) 'Local clusters and local export growth', *New Zealand Strategic Management,* Summer: 24-30

Ffowcs Williams, I (1997b) 'Upgrading Nelson, New Zealand's seafood capital', *Seafood New Zealand,* June: 35-9

Field A, S Goldfinch and M Perry (1994) *Promoting Small Business Networking an Agency Comparison*, Economic Restructuring and Skill Development Research Report 2, Wellington: New Zealand Institute for Social Research and Development

Film Wellington (1999) 'The Wellington film industry – what it is worth', *Film Wellington Newsclip*, September

Firth, M (1987) 'Multiple directorships and corporate interlocks in New Zealand', *Australia-New Zealand Journal of Sociology* 23: 274-81

Fogelberg, G and C Laurent (1973) 'Interlocking directorates: a study of large companies in New Zealand', *Journal of Business Policy* 3: 16-21

Frame, D (2000) 'Finland and New Zealand: A Cross Country Comparison of Economic Performance', Treasury Working Paper 00/1, Wellington: New Zealand Treasury

Frater P, G Andrews, G Stuart and F Harris (1998) *The Driver Clusters of the Nelson Region Economy*, Report prepared for Nelson City Council, Tasman District Council, Port Nelson Ltd and Nelson Regional Airport Authority, Wellington: Business and Economic Research Ltd

Fukuyama, F (1992) *The End of History and the Last Man*, New York: The Free Press

Gould, J (1982) *The Rake's Progress? The New Zealand Economy Since 1945*, Auckland: Hodder and Stoughton

Granovetter, M (1992) 'Problems of explanation in economic sociology', in N

Nohria and R Eccles (eds) *Networks and Organizations: Structure, Form and Action,* Boston: Harvard Business School Press

Grant, W (1993) *Business and Politics in Britain,* London: Macmillan

Green, K (1985) *Research Funding in Australia: A View From the North,* Canberra: Department of Science

Grupp, H (1995) 'Science, high technology and the competitiveness of EU countries', *Cambridge Journal of Economics* 19: 209-223

Gustafson, B (1986) *From the Cradle to the Grave. A Bibliography of Michael Joseph Savage,* Auckland: Reed Methuen

Hawke, G (1985) *The Making of New Zealand,* Cambridge: Cambridge University Press

Hawke, G (1997) *The Thoroughbred Among Banks in New Zealand: 1872-1947 The Early Years,* Wellington: National Bank of New Zealand

Hayward, D (1996) 'Industrial concentration and industry strategy', in R Le Heron and E Pawson (eds) *Changing Places: New Zealand in the Nineties,* Auckland: Longman Paul

Healy, P (1997) 'Peter Healy reports', *Hard Business Networks Newsletter,* Wellington: New Zealand Trade Development Board, November

Henriksen, L (1995) 'Formal cooperation among firms in networks: the case of Danish joint ventures and strategic alliances', *European Planning Studies* 3 (2): 254-60

Herrigel, G (1989) 'Industrial order and the politics of industrial change: mechanical engineering', in P Katzenstein (ed.) *Industry and Politics in West Germany: Toward the Third Republic,* Ithaca and London: Cornell University Press

Hirst, P and G Thompson (1996) *Globalization in Question,* Cambridge: Polity Press

Holt, L (1986) *Compulsory Arbitration in New Zealand: The First Forty Years,* Auckland: Auckland University Press

Huggins, R (1996) 'Technology policy, networks and small firms in Denmark', *Regional Studies* 30: 523-52

Jesson, B (1979) 'The business elite of Auckland', *The Republican* 26: 9-14

Jesson, B (1992) 'Lobbying and protest: patterns of political change at the informal level', in H Gold (ed.) *New Zealand Politics in Perspective,* Third edition, Auckland: Longman Paul

Jesson, B (1999) *Only Their Purpose is Mad,* Palmerston North: Dunmore Press

Katzenstein, PJ (1985) *Small States in World Markets. Industrial Policy in Europe,* Ithaca: Cornell University Press

Kenney, M and R Florida (1993) *Beyond Mass Production,* New York: Oxford University Press

Korkman, S (1992) 'Exchange rate policy and employment in small open economies', in J Pekkarinen, M Pohjola and B Rowthorn (eds) *Social*

Corporatism: A Superior Economic System, Oxford: Clarendon Press

Knuckey S, L-W Jason and M Meskill (1999) *Gearing Up – A Study of Best Manufacturing Practice in New Zealand*, Wellington: Ministry of Commerce

Kristensen P, (1996) 'On the constitution of economic actors in Denmark', in R Whitley and P Kristensen (eds) *The Changing European Firm – Limits to Convergence*, London: Routledge

Kristensen P, K Lilja and R Tainio (1996)'Comparing typical firms in Denmark and Finland', in R Whitley and P Kristensen (eds) *The Changing European Firm – Limits to Convergence*, London: Routledge

Landesmann, M and J Vartianen (1992) 'Social corporatism and long term economic performance', in J Pekkarinen, M Pohjola and B Rowthorn (eds) *Social Corporatism: A Superior Economic System*, Oxford: Clarendon Press

Le Heron, R (1980) 'The diversified corporation and development strategy – New Zealand's experience', *Regional Studies* 14 (3): 201-18

Lilja K, K Rasanen and R Tainio (1992) 'A dominant business recipe: the forest sector in Finland', in R Whitley (ed.) *European Business Systems Firms and Markets in their National Contexts*, London: Sage

Lilja, K and R Tainio (1996) 'The nature of the typical Finnish firm', in R Whitley and P Kristensen (eds) *The Changing European Firm – Limits to Convergence*, London: Routledge

Mabbett, D (1995) *Trade, Employment, and Welfare: A Comparative Study of Trade and Labour Market Policies in Sweden and New Zealand, 1880-1980*, Oxford: Clarendon Press

Maher, P (1996) 'Hard business networks: a comparative study', unpublished Master of Business Administration thesis, Auckland: Graduate School of Business, University of Auckland

Malecki, E (1997) *Technology and Economic Development*, Harlow: Longman

Marceau, J (1992) 'Small country business systems: Australia, Denmark and Finland compared', in R Whitley (ed.) *European Business Systems Firms and Markets in their National Contexts*, London: Sage

Masaki, N (1998) 'Ownership and control of large corporations in contemporary Japan', in H Harukiyo and G Hook (eds) *Japanese Business Management: Restructuring for Low Growth and Globalization*, London: Routledge.

Maskell, P (1998) 'Learning in the village economy of Denmark: the role of institutions and policy in sustaining competitiveness', in H-J Braczyk, P Cooke and M Heidenreich (eds) *Regional Innovation Systems*, London: UCL Press

Maskell P, H Eskelin, I Hannibalsson, A Malmberg and E Vatne (1998) *Competitiveness Localised Learning and Regional Development*, London: Routledge

McCann, D (1995) *Small States, Open Markets and the Organization of Business Interests*, Aldershot: Avebury

Ministry of Research Science and Technology (1998) *Building Tomorrow's Success: Guidelines for Thinking Beyond Today*, Wellington: Ministry of Research Science and Technology

de la Mothe, J and G Pasquet (1996) *Evolutionary Economics and the New International Political Economy*, Pinter, London

Nielsen, K and O Pedersen (1988) 'The negotiated economy: ideal and history', *Scandinavian Political Studies* 11 (2): 79-101

Nielsen, K and O Pedersen (1991) 'From the mixed economy to the negotiated economy: the Scandinavian countries', in R Coughlin (ed.) *Morality, Rationality and Efficiency: New Perspectives on Socio-Economics*, New York: M E Sharpe

Organisation of Economic Cooperation and Development (OECD) (1985) *Social Expenditure 1960-1990: Problems of Growth and Control*, Paris: Organisation of Economic Cooperation and Development

Organisation of Economic Cooperation and Development (OECD) (1995) *Boosting Business Advisory Services*, Paris: Organisation of Economic Cooperation and Development

Organisation of Economic Cooperation and Development (OECD) (1996) *Networks of Enterprises and Local Development*, Paris: Organisation for Economic Cooperation and Development

Organisation of Economic Cooperation and Development (OECD) (1998) *The OECD STAN Database for Industrial Analysis 1978-1997*, Paris: Organisation of Economic Cooperation and Development

Organisation of Economic Cooperation and Development (OECD) (1999) *OECD Science, Technology and Industry Scoreboard 1999 Benchmarking Knowledge-Based Economies*, Paris: Organisation of Economic Cooperation and Development

Oliver, W H (1989) 'The Labour caucus and economic policy formation, 1981-1984', in B Easton (ed.) *The Making of Rogernomics*, Auckland: Auckland University Press

Olssen, E (1992) 'Towards a new society' in G Rice (ed.) *The Oxford History of New Zealand*, Auckland: Oxford University Press

Pedersen, O (1992) 'The institutional history of the Danish polity', in S-E Sjostrand (ed.) *Institutional Change. Theoretical Considerations and Empirical Findings*, New York: M E Sharpe

Pedersen O, N Andersen and P Kjaer (1992) 'Private policies and the autonomy of enterprise: Danish local and national industrial policy', *Journal of Economic Issues* 26 (4): 1117-44

Pekkarinen, J (1992) 'Corporatism and economic performance in Sweden, Norway and Finland', in J Pekkarinen, M Pohjola and B Rowthorn (eds) *Social Corporatism: A Superior Economic System*, Oxford: Clarendon Press

Perry, M (1995) 'Industry structures, networks and joint action groups', *Regional*

Studies 29 (3): 208-217

Perry, M (1999) *Small Firms and Network Economies*, London: Routledge

Perry M, C Davidson and R Hill (1995) *Reform at Work*, Auckland: Longman Paul

Perry M, R Le Heron, D Hayward and I Cooper (1997) 'Growing discipline through total quality management in a New Zealand horticulture region', *Journal of Rural Studies* 13 (3): 289-304

Porter, M (1990) *The Competitive Advantage of Nations*, New York: Free Press

Putnam, R with R Leonardi and R Nanetti (1993) *Making Democracy Work. Civic Traditions in Modern Italy*, Princeton: Princeton University Press

Robinson, D (1997) *Social Capital and Policy Development*, Wellington: Institute of Policy Studies

Roper, B (1993) 'A level playing field? Business activism and state policy formation', in B Roper and C Rudd (eds) *State and Economy in New Zealand*, Auckland: Oxford University Press

Sabel, C (1994) 'Learning by monitoring: the institutions of economic development', in N Smelser and R Swedberg (eds) *The Handbook of Economic Sociology*, Princeton: Princeton University Press

Sako, M (1992) *Prices, Quality and Trust: Inter-firm Relations in Britain and Japan*, Cambridge: Cambridge University Press

Schienstock G, P Koskiand P Rasanen (1998) 'The regionalization of the Finnish innovation system: the case of Pirkanmaa', in H-J Braczyk, P Cooke and M Heidenreich (eds) *Regional Innovation Systems*, London: UCL Press

Sharp, M (1998) 'Fishing', in A Bollard (ed.) *The Structure and Dynamics of New Zealand Industries*, Palmerston North: Dunmore Press

Skully, M (1985) *Financial Institutions and Markets in the Southwest Pacific*, London: Macmillan

Spellerberg, A (1997) 'Towards a framework for the measurement of social capital', in D Robinson (ed.) *Social Capital and Policy Development*, Wellington: Institute of Policy Studies

Spring, D (1992) 'An international marketer's view of Porter's New Zealand study', *Business Quarterly* 56 (Winter): 65-69

Trade New Zealand (1996) *Stretching for Growth: Two Years Into an Eight Year Journey*, Wellington: New Zealand Trade Development Board

Uriu, R (1996) *Troubled Industries: Confronting Economic Change in Japan*, Ithaca and London: Cornell University Press

Vitalis, A and R Walker (1992) 'Productivity and management – a New Zealand perspective' in I A Pappas and I P Tatsiopoulos (eds) *Advances in Production Management Systems*, Netherlands, Elsevier Science Publishers

Vowles, J (1992) 'Business, unions and the state: organising economic interests in New Zealand' in H Gold (ed.) *New Zealand Politics in Perspective*, Third edition, Auckland: Longman Paul

Vowles, J and J Roper (1997) 'Business and politics during the postwar era', in C Rudd and B Roper (eds) *The Political Economy of New Zealand*, Auckland: Oxford University Press

Walker, G and L Poppo (1991) 'Profit centres, single-source suppliers, and transaction costs', *Administrative Science Quarterly* 36: 66-87

Walsh, P (1988) 'Technology and the competitiveness of small countries: review', in C Van Freeman and B-A Lundvall (eds) *Small Countries Facing the Technological Revolutions*, London: Pinter

Wanna, J (1989) 'Centralisation without corporatism: the politics of New Zealand business in the recession', *New Zealand Journal of Industrial Relations* 14 (1): 1-15

Whitley, R (1992) *Business Systems in East Asia: Firms, Markets and Societies*, London: Sage

Whitley, R (1999) *Divergent Capitalisms: The Social Structuring and Change of Business Systems*, Oxford: Oxford University Press

Williamson, 0 (1994) 'Transaction cost economics and organization theory', in N Smelser and R Swedberg (eds) *The Handbook of Economic Sociology*, Princeton: Princeton University Press

World Bank (1997) *Expanding the Measure of Wealth, Environmentally Sustainable Development*, Studies and Monographs Series Number 17, Washington: World Bank

Yetton P, J Craig, J Davis and F Hilmer (1992) 'Are diamonds a country's best fried? A critique of Porter's theory of national competition as applied to Canada, New Zealand and Australia', *Australia Journal of Management* 17 (1): 1-32 *c   o   n   t*

4 INTRODUCTION
PAGE
- The aims of this book and how to measure and record your pain

6 WHAT IS PAIN and HOW CAN TENS AFFECT IT?
PAGE
- How we feel pain and how stimulation of the large nerves can reduce it

8 THE TENS MACHINE
PAGE
- Important notes, how to select the right machine and electrodes

10 WHERE TO PLACE THE ELECTRODES
PAGE
- Nerves, nerve roots and dermatomes explained
- How to locate the vertebrae

13 DERMATOME MAPS
PAGE
- An illustrative guide to the body's dermatome areas

16 USING THE TENS MACHINE
PAGE
- How to set and adjust the TENS unit and position the electrodes correctly
- Daily routines for administering treatment
- What to expect from your TENS machine
- Increasing activity during the periods of less pain
- The endorphin alternative
- Exploring high and low frequencies
- Common problems which affect good pain management

22 SOME COMMON PROBLEMS
PAGE
- How to deal with some of the most common problems of TENS usage

24 EXAMPLES of ELECTRODE PLACEMENT
PAGE
- An illustrative guide to electrode placement for common pain symptoms

34 ELECTRODE PLACEMENTS for NAUSEA
PAGE
- An illustrative guide to electrode placement for nausea

35 ELECTRODE PLACEMENTS for MIGRAINE
PAGE
- An illustrative guide to electrode placement for migraine

Introduction

THE 'TENS' UNIT

Chronic pain is one of the most difficult 'conditions' to treat. Family doctors may find it frustrating as they exhaust their armoury of medication without making any significant progress on alleviating their patients' pain. The patient too becomes frustrated and, if the pain is persistent, they can begin to develop signs of anxiety and stress.

Long-term pain sufferers often turn to complementary therapies and non-prescription remedies in their search for a solution to the misery of prolonged pain. You may have seen the many newspaper and magazine advertisements which offer 'pain relief without drugs'. This may be achieved through using Transcutaneous Electrical Nerve Stimulation, ('TENS').

IMPROVING INFORMATION

TENS can be very effective in treating both chronic and acute pain. However, it is not a case of simply applying electrodes and switching on the machine. Many people who have tried TENS unsuccessfully needed only a few simple instructions on how to use the device properly in order to achieve the results they were looking for. Unfortunately, there are very few instruction books supplied with TENS units which cover the subject adequately. In addition, there may be a few clinicians who are unsure how to get the most from TENS units and consequently pass inaccurate information to patients. However, the electrode positions described in this book illustrate only one of the ways of using TENS, so don't be worried if your health professionals employ different positions. If you are using TENS without the support of a health professional, follow the guide in the coming pages.

This booklet addresses the problem of insufficient or inaccurate information. Designed to be easily understood without prior medical knowledge, it explains what pain is and how TENS can help, offers guidance on one method of positioning electrodes, suggests how to select the most suitable machine and includes advice on operating and adjusting the unit to maximise its effectiveness.

ABOUT THIS BOOK

Take some time to read through all of this book carefully and follow the steps given as a plan of action. You will find that TENS will not cure your pain, but it should make life tolerable again. The clinic where the author practiced has carried out many studies in the effectiveness of TENS and 80% of users report significant benefit from using it.

All of these people received regular instruction on how to position the electrodes and adjust their machine correctly. To achieve the same results, you should follow the instructions in this manual accurately. Don't forget, if you are working under the care of a health professional, they may employ slightly different electrode positions than those described in this booklet.

The writer has attempted to keep this text concise in order to encourage you to read and reread the contents. If the subject was simple, this book wouldn't be necessary but be patient - remember that the best person to treat your pain with TENS is YOU! Don't be tempted to skip parts of the book; you will only obtain the best performance from your machine if you understand fully how TENS interacts with the nervous system and pain.

MEASURING PAIN

Measuring pain is an essential part of managing it. Pre-treatment levels are required to assess the most effective method of treatment so before you move on to the next page, you should use the following guide to gauge your level of pain and write down your pain score.

Imagine that a score of '0' represents no pain at all and a score of '10' is the worst pain imaginable. Write down the number from 1 to 10 that best describes your pain (a) at its MOST in a single week, and (b) at its LEAST in a single week.

If you find it difficult to imagine your pain in these terms, try drawing a straight line of 10 cm. Write 'least pain' at one end and 'worst pain' at the other and mark the line at the point you consider reflects the strength of your pain at its most in a week and its least in a week. You can now take a ruler and measure the distance from the point marked 'least pain' to the mark which represents your pain level and note down the number in centimetres.

You can also make a note of how far and for how long you can comfortably walk or perform some other form of activity which is affected by your pain, eg. vacuuming, driving, ironing etc.

Put these scores on one side for the moment. We'll return to them once we've used the TENS machine.

What is pain?
and how can TENS affect it?

TYPES OF PAIN

Pain is usually a warning that something is wrong with our body - it's an urgent message to prevent us from damaging our tissue further. We often respond to new or **acute pain** by withdrawing our hand or foot from the danger in order to limit the damage it will cause. If, for example, we were to twist an ankle, the pain would prevent us from running and if the ankle were to be badly sprained, even walking would be inhibited. This acute pain limits use of the damaged ankle until the injury has had time to heal sufficiently and so acute pain as a symptom of injury can actually be beneficial.

Under normal circumstances, as the damaged tissue repairs itself, the pain gradually lessens until we are no longer aware of it and can continue walking, running etc. quite normally. However, there are occasions when pain continues beyond the time taken for tissue to heal. When this occurs, the pain is no longer a symptom but a problem in its own right. This type of pain is referred to as **chronic pain**. It is not necessary to have suffered an injury to experience chronic pain - it may even arise following 'successful' surgery. This 'untreatable' pain is sometimes associated with diseases such as arthritis or simple wear and tear of the body.

From a medical point of view, pain doesn't show up on x-rays, ultrasound scans or even Magnetic Resonance Imaging (MRI). Without any physical evidence, both patient and doctor can suspect that the pain is actually imagined.

HOW DO WE FEEL PAIN?

The pain message is transmitted from the injured area via some of the smallest of the body's nerve fibres to the spinal cord and then on to the brain which translates the messages and makes us 'feel' the pain. The painful sensations are 'remoted' to the injured area so that if we burn our hand, we quickly withdraw the hand rather than pulling back our head.

There are millions upon millions of small nerve fibres throughout the body and it may only require around five impulses a second in five nerve cells to produce chronic pain. Imagine then how difficult it can be to trace the source of a patient's chronic pain - it makes the search for the Holy Grail look a soft option in comparison!

LARGE DIAMETER NERVE FIBRES

In addition to the small nerve fibres which allow the sensation of pain to be felt, the human body is also equipped with thicker nerve fibres. These carry less unpleasant sensations such as warmth, touch and the position of our joints, helping us to form an impression of our environment. The sensation of touch is particularly relevant when considering pain, since as we know, anywhere in the world, if someone accidentally knocks their elbow, they instinctively rub it. This rubbing action excites the larger nerve fibres which, in turn, have an effect on the transmission of signals from the smaller 'pain-carrying' nerves. It seems the benefit of stimulating greater activity in the larger nerve fibres may be fourfold:

1. The speed of small nerve cell transmission is reduced
2. The amount of information transmitted from the small nerves to the spinal cord is reduced (known as the 'Pain-gate')
3. Under certain circumstances, the brain will produce its own pain-killing substance (known as endorphins or endogenous opioids)
4. The production of Dynorphins

The ancient Egyptians explored this phenomenon without understanding what was happening in the nerves. Hieroglyphics discovered, illustrate a practice of standing sufferers of painful gout on electric eels. We may be better athletes today, but performing a balancing act on a slippery eel would still be beyond most of us!

In 1969, the scientists Melzack and Wall described something called the 'Pain-gate' (see point 2 above). The theory of the pain gate lead to the development of TENS units designed specifically to stimulate the large diameter nerve fibres.

Don't rush off and buy or try your TENS machine yet. The next section in the book explains how to select a suitable machine, how to set and operate it and where to place the electrodes. This is all essential information that you should know before proceeding to use the equipment.

The TENS Machine

IMPORTANT NOTES

YOU SHOULD NOT USE A TENS MACHINE:

- If you have a pacemaker fitted
- If you are in the first three months of pregnancy do not place electrodes on the trunk or pelvis
- If your skin is broken or fragile where the electrodes are to be placed
- Whilst driving or operating machinery
- Over insensitive skin
- If the wearer suffers from epilepsy they should not be alone when using TENS. If they suffer a seizure, the intensity may be accidentally increased thus causing skin damage

SELECTING A TENS MACHINE

There are many different types of TENS unit on the market and various sources for acquiring them. They can be purchased by mail order, via specialists shops and chemists, or directly from the manufacturer or importer of the unit.

You should be aware that some units are restricted in their scope of output combinations and consequently may limit the potential for trying various options. This can be a crucial factor in finding the best output required to control your particular pain. Be wary of fantastic claims and exaggerated lists of what the supplier says the TENS can treat.

The following guide provides a profile of the optimum TENS machines. You may not require any more from your unit, but you must not accept anything less.

STANDARD TENS UNIT

1. The unit should be small enough to wear comfortably on the belt whilst on the move
2. There should be two outlets, each accepting one pair of wires. Each outlet should in turn have its own control knob to enable independent adjustment of the current. The machine should therefore drive four electrodes.
3. The unit should include features enabling you to:
   - adjust pulse width - most units will have at least 80 to 220 micro seconds variability
   - adjust pulse rate or frequency - 2 to 150 hertz allowing a gradual increase between these outputs
   - switch between 'constant' and 'burst'
   - have two separate, easily accessible intensity controls giving between 0 and 80 mA into a 500 Ohm load or 0-60 mA into a 1500 Ohm load

MIXED FREQUENCY TENS UNIT

There is also a new type of machine which is programmable to provide the outputs described above. In addition to these, there are programmes of mixed frequency which switch automatically between low and high frequencies. It is suggested that this type of stimulation may encourage the simultaneous release of both endorphins and dynorphins or endorphin release and pain gate closure.

Don't worry if you don't understand - all will become clear as you read on. For the moment, all you need to do is continue reading and then refer to the features above when you are ready to buy a machine.

ELECTRODES

The electrodes are the flexible pads which are placed against the skin and connected to the TENS machine by thin wires which carry the current from the unit to the pads. The current then excites the underlying nerves.
There are basically two types of electrode:

- a rubber electrode which is smeared with conductive gel and held in the appropriate place with sticky tape, eg. Micropore
- self-adhesive electrodes which are pre-coated with a sticky gel which conducts electricity

Of the two types, the self-adhesive type is much easier to use, though they may be slightly more expensive. Your supplier should be able to offer you spares for both wires and electrodes as they both wear out in time.

In this manual, we will refer to 'black' and 'red' electrodes. In the method of treatment described in this booklet, the black electrode or cathode is known as the 'distal' electrode and is connected via the black wire to the TENS unit. The red electrode or anode is called the 'proximal' electrode and is connected to the unit by a red wire.

You must NOT place electrodes over the front of the neck - this can cause problems with blood pressure!

Figure 1.

NERVES

If you imagine a tree without its leaves and positioned upside down, this resembles the body's nervous system, (see *Figures. 1 and 2*) The roots (now at the top) represent the brain; the trunk represents the spinal cord and the branches and twigs of the tree are like the peripheral nerves which gradually become thinner as they reach the furthest points of your limbs. The nerves are more symmetrical than the random order of branches in a tree but this illustration gives you some idea of how the nervous system is structured.

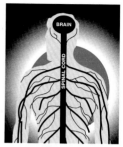

Figure 2.

Specific parts of the body are served not only by specific nerves, but each nerve has its own 'entrance' into the spinal column and then into the spinal cord. Earlier, I referred to the importance of stimulating the larger nerves in order to 'block' the painful impulses in the smaller nerves. The fact that the two belong to the same group is critical. If your pain is deduced as being carried along the sciatic nerve for example, then this is the nerve which should be stimulated with the TENS unit and hence one of the black electrodes should be placed at some point along the length of this nerve.

NERVE ROOTS

Before explaining where to place the second electrode, we should undderstand what a nerve root is. *Figure 3* shows part of the spinal cord viewed from behind. If you feel one of the bony vertebra that lay under the skin running down the centre of your neck or back and then move your finger a couple of centimetres to the left or right, your finger will now be over the nerve root for that level of your spine. The nerve root is the first part of the nerve just outside the spinal cord. There are eight pairs of nerve roots in the neck (or cervical region), twelve pairs in the upper back (or thoracic region), five pairs in the lower back (or lumbar region), and five pairs in the pelvic (or sacral) area.

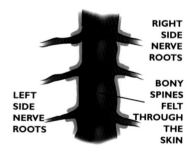

Figure 3. *Spinal Cord from behind*

Returning to the example of the sciatic nerve, a suitable place for the red electrode may be over one of the nerve roots which serves this particular nerve. Note that there are two nerve roots at each level of the spine, one entering from the left and the other from the right. If you had placed the first electrode on your left leg, then the second electrode must be placed over the nerve root on the same side. This will all become clearer as you read on.

DERMATOMES

A dermatome describes an area of the skin which is served by a single nerve root. As most of us are constructed in more or less the same way, anatomists have mapped out a body diagram of where the dermatomes are positioned across the body. The illustrations on page 13-15 show the location of the dermatomes. These maps will assist us later when deciding where to place the electrodes to treat your pain.

UNDERSTANDING DERMATOMES

Each nerve root serves a known area of the skin. This area is not exclusive - there is no fine line separating the borders between dermatomes but rather, each area contains a certain amount of overlap across adjacent areas. The dermatomes are named after the nerve root which serves it and the following table describes how the dermatomes are designated.

C1 to C8	Neck or cervical spine
T1 to T12	Chest or thorax
L1 to L5	Lower back or lumbar spine
S1 to S5	Pelvis or sacrum

If your pain does not radiate into one of the limbs and is confined to the spine, you may not need to know the dermatomes. For information on where to place the electrodes for spine pain, see page 17.

If a major part of your pain is located away from the spine, for example, down the back of your leg, you must be able to identify and find the nerve root that serves this area so that you can place the red electrode in the correct position. The black electrode, as you will remember, is placed at a point along the length of the nerve between the spine and the pain, usually just on the spinal side of the pain and sometimes directly over it.

Placing the black (distal) electrode is relatively easy - you are guided by your pain. To place the red (proximal) electrode, you must first identify the dermatome associated with your pain. Use the illustrations on pages 13-15 to locate the area in which the pain is felt and write down the letter and number corresponding to the dermatome identified for this area. We now need to find the appropriate vertebra alongside which you will place the red electrode. Thankfully, rather like the pubs that people use to describe a route when giving directions, there are a few landmarks to guide us.

LOCATING THE VERTEBRAE

The Neck
If you drop your chin towards your chest, a lump will rise in the middle of the back of your neck, almost level with your shoulders. This is C7. Count the vertebrae up from this to find the one you need and you will locate the desired nerve root.

The Chest
T1 is the next vertebra below C7. If you place your arms by your sides and ask someone to find the vertebra which lies midway between the lowest points of your shoulder blades, this vertebra is T7. Again, you can count up from T7 or down from T1 to locate the desired vertebra and nerve root. In practice, if your pain is on the front or side of your chest, place the black electrode over the pain, or at the spinal side of the pain. Then follow the rib line to the spine and place the red electrode alongside the spine.

The Lower Back
Place your hands on your hips and feel firmly up and down until you locate the upper-most brim of the pelvis. The vertebra in the middle of the back between these two points is L4. Count upwards to find vertebrae L3 to L1 or down one vertebra to locate L5.

Don't be too concerned if you have difficulty finding the vertebrae - it soon becomes second nature. With practice, you will be able to place your electrodes with skill and sound reason. It is important to remember that this is YOUR PAIN and that it's in YOUR INTEREST to get it right. If the electrodes are placed incorrectly, the wrong nerves will be treated and the maximum possible benefit may not be achieved.

At the back of the book, (pages 24 - 33) there are a number of 'body charts' showing examples for the most common problems of pain with some suggested electrode positions. Don't forget, if you are under the care of a health professional, they may decide to use different electrode positions than those described at the back of this booklet. If these work for you, stick with them.

Dermatome Maps 1

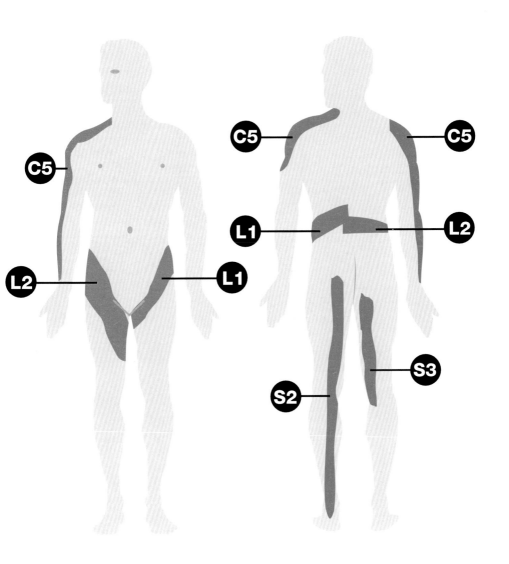

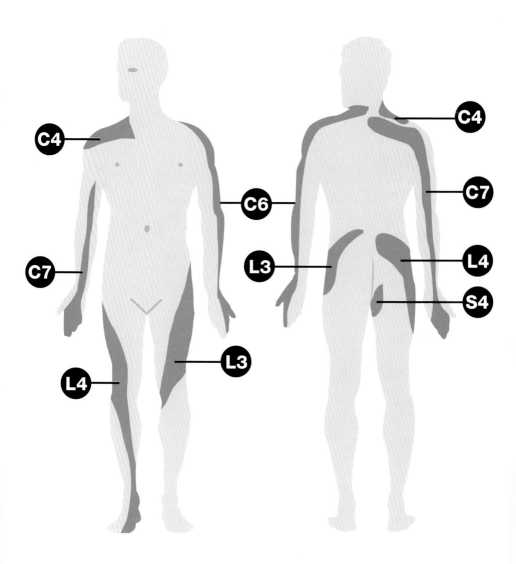

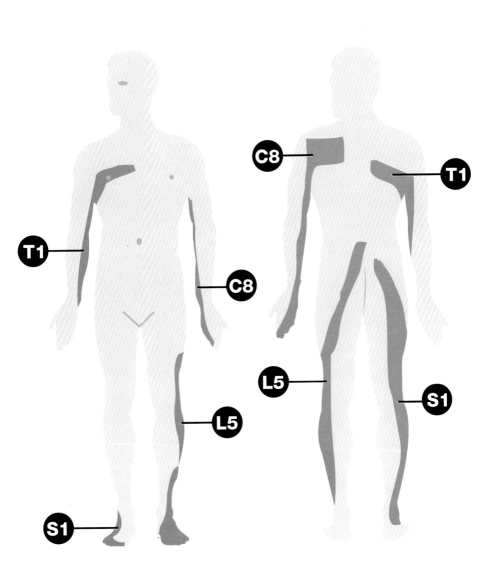

We now need a plan to follow - a logical progression in setting and then adjusting the TENS machine. Don't forget that we are not looking for a miracle cure, but a significant reduction in pain. Temporary analgesia is probably the best way to describe a good result.

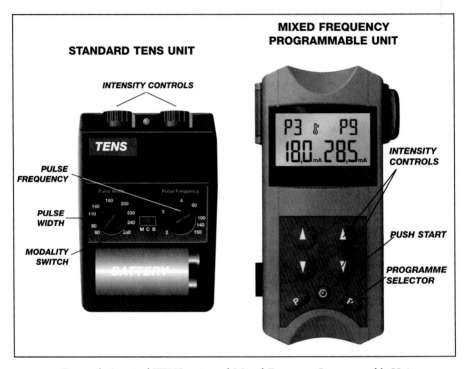

Figure 4. *A typical TENS unit and Mixed Frequency Programmable Unit*

The first part of this book described how stimulating the large nerves affected the transmission of the small, pain-carrying nerves. How you set the machine will determine whether pain is managed by 'pain-gating' (reducing the amount of painful impulses transmitted by the spinal cord to the brain) or by encouraging the brain to produce the natural painkillers - endorphins.

Figure 4. shows typical units and the available adjustment options. If your machine is different to the examples shown, examine the instructions that accompanied the machine that you are using in order to identify the position of each switch.

The first, and usually the most successful method of pain control is that which stimulates pain-gating\dynorphin production. It requires the following setting on your TENS unit:

1. Set the Pulse Width to 180 – 200 microseconds
2. Set the Modality switch to 'C' or CONSTANT or if your machine is marked 'N' for NORMAL, use this setting. (There will usually be Burst and Modulated options too)
3. Set the Frequency (or Pulse Rate) to 80 Hz

Set your machine as described above. If you have a programmable machine, select the programme which provides the settings described above. The next stage is to decide where to place the electrodes.

POSITIONING THE ELECTRODES

Refer back to the illustrations of dermatomes on pages 13-15. Remember that these are the areas of the skin which are supplied by certain nerve roots. Locate the correct dermatome by marking the picture carefully at the point where your main pain is felt. This will help to guide you when positioning the electrodes.

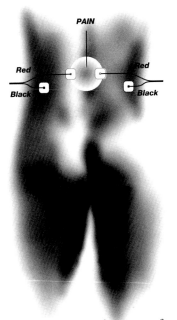

As a general guide, the electrode connected to the red lead should be placed alongside the spine where the dermatome (on which your pain lies) enters/exits the spine. (see *Figure 2*). The electrode connected to the black lead should be placed either directly over your pain or closer to the spine within the dermatome where the pain is felt. Make sure that both electrodes are placed on the same side of your body and that the electrodes are not connected to the machine at this stage.

If your pain is felt on both sides of the body, you will need to use both sets of leads and four electrodes - one pair on the left and the

Figure 5. Electrode Positions for Controlling Lower Back Pain

other pair on the right. If your pain is in the middle of your back, you will also need to use both pairs of electrodes in the position shown in *Figure 5*.

SWITCHING ON

Once the electrodes are correctly positioned with the lead connected to each one, you are then ready to connect them to the unit. Make sure that the unit is switched off before doing this.

After checking that the unit settings are as described on page 17, you can switch the unit on. Increase the intensity control until you can feel a strong but comfortable tingling sensation under at least one of each pair of electrodes. If you can feel a tingle under both electrodes of the pair or pairs being used, this is acceptable but not necessary for pain management.

Congratulations! You have now taken the first step in taking charge of your pain.

A DAILY ROUTINE

Continue to take all of your medication for the moment. If you have good results using the TENS machine, you may be able to reduce your medication in the future. You should discuss this with your doctor after about one month of using TENS.

Whilst using TENS, your day should follow the routine described below:

- Before positioning the electrodes in the morning, you must wash and dry your skin. If you shower or bathe in the mornings, there is no need for further skin cleaning. This practice ensures a good electrical contact, extends the life of the electrodes and reduces the risk of skin irritation.

- Place the electrodes in the correct positions.

- Switch your machine on and adjust the intensity control until you feel a comfortable tingle. DON'T be tempted to turn the intensity up too high, as this may stimulate the small nerves and make your pain worse!

- After 20 minutes or so, you may find that the tingling sensation has gone. If this is the case, gradually increase the intensity until you can feel a comfortable tingle again.

- Continue with your machine switched on for a total of 1-1^1/$_2$ hours. Each 1-1^1/$_2$ hour session constitutes a treatment. You may consider leaving the electrodes in place between treatments. Many people can tolerate this. However, if you experience skin irritation, remove the electrodes after each treatment.

- Repeat the 1-1^1/$_2$ hour treatments four times each day. This will administer a total maximum daily treatment of six hours. Choose the times to coincide with your periods of activity or 'worst pain'. If you have a problem sleeping due to your pain, try to save one of your treatments for the hour and a half before you go to bed.

- Before going to bed, remove the electrodes and place them back onto the plastic or paper backing that they were supplied with. Read the instructions that accompanied the TENS electrodes, as some manufacturers recommend storing the electrodes in a refrigerator overnight.

- Continue with the above routine for at least one week unless you experience any problems during treatment. After one week, re-score your pain to assess how effective the TENS is managing it.

WHAT TO EXPECT

After using your machine for about 20 minutes, your pain should gradually lessen. Don't expect it to disappear completely or you may be disappointed. Of the 450 people seen each year in the clinic where the author practiced, only 3 or 4 experienced complete resolution of their pain whereas 80% experienced a significant reduction in their pain. This allows them to live a much fuller life as a result.

After switching off the TENS, your pain may steadily return over a variable period of time - this is known as 'carry-over'. Depending on the individual, the carry-over period may last for anything from minutes to days. You may feel that the pain is not as severe when it begins to return but unless you continue to apply regular stimulation with your TENS, it may eventually return to its former glory. If the carry-over period is significantly long, then TENS treatments may be reduced to every other day.

Don't forget to return to the pain scoring technique described on page 5 in order to assess the effectiveness of the treatment. Do this before looking at the score you gave a week ago, then compare the two scores. Is it better, worse or still the same? If the pain score is halved during the use of TENS, this is considered a good result.

INCREASING ACTIVITY

Effective TENS treatments will provide you with a 'window' in which your pain is more tolerable. Don't be afraid to **slowly** increase your activity during these periods. Remember the difference between acute and chronic pain - acute pain is designed to prevent movement during healing whereas in chronic pain syndromes, all healing has taken place. It is natural to be cautious of becoming more active, but fear of movement will cause you more problems than movement itself.

THE ENDORPHIN ALTERNATIVE

If, after a week of using the TENS regularly, where you have faithfully followed the instructions on the preceding pages, you do not experience good pain management, it may be necessary to try managing the pain using endorphin production, (see point 3 of the table on page 7). This will require adjustment of your TENS unit as follows: (Remember to disconnect the unit from the electrode wires before adjusting the settings)

> **1.** Leave the Pulse Width setting at 180 – 200 microseconds
> **2.** Set the Modality switch to 'B' or BURST
> **3.** Increase the Frequency (or Pulse Rate) to 100 Hz

At the above settings, you will find the sensation 'pulsing' rather than the 'tingling' that you have experienced so far. On some machines, the lights may also pulsate.

Using the machine on its new settings, you should follow the same course as previously described, ie. 4 times a day for 1-1^1/$_2$ hours each time. Again, continue treatments for a week before you make further adjustments, unless problems arise.

After one week, re-score your pain again and compare the score with that taken before TENS treatments began and with that taken after using TENS on the 'constant' or 'normal' setting. Don't forget that even with TENS, you will still experience good and bad days - be sure to record the **average** score.

There is an exception to using only low intensities of stimulation. If you have not achieved pain management on the 'Burst' setting so far, leave your machine on the Burst setting but increase the intensity until you can see a muscle twitch under the black (distal) electrode. Continue with this level of stimulation for **TWENTY TO THIRTY MINUTES**. Repeat this treatment three times per day, giving a total treatment time of between one hour and one hour and a half per day.
This is not the most comfortable treatments but it can sometimes prove very effective.

Is your TENS more effective with the new settings? If the answer is 'yes', continue with the plan using the new settings. If the answer is 'no', return to the constant modality setting that you started with and explore low and high frequencies using the instructions on the following page.

If, however, you have purchased a mixed frequency machine, you may consider using one of the programmes which will provide ether 15/2 Hz or 80/2Hz stimulation. Try each of these programmes for 5-7 days before re-assessing.

EXPLORING LOW and HIGH FREQUENCIES

1. Leave the Pulse Width setting at 200 microseconds
2. Set the Modality switch to 'C' or CONSTANT or if your machine is marked 'N' for NORMAL, use this setting
3. Set the Frequency (or Pulse Rate) to 50 Hz for 4 days. If a good result is achieved, continue to use the machine at this setting. If not, try resetting the frequency to between 4-30Hz for the next three days.

Try using your TENS on the above settings for a week and then reassess the pain score again. If you are still not achieving reasonable pain management:

Change the Frequency (or Pulse Rate) to 120 or 150 Hz for 1 week and then reassess.

COMMON FACTORS WHICH AFFECT GOOD PAIN MANAGEMENT

- Incorrect positioning of electrodes. Even if you start with them in the right place, you must replace them **accurately** each time that you use them.
- Not using the TENS for the correct periods. Remember that treatments should last for 1-1 1/2 hours and be carried out 4 times each day.
- Turning up the machine's intensity too high.
- Returning to activity too quickly. Good pain management depends on you returning to activity **slowly**.
- Caffine: Research has indicated that the amount of caffine found in 2-3 cups of coffee may be sufficient to block the pain relieving effects of TENS. This may not apply to decaffinated tea and coffee.

Some Common Problems

SKIN REACTION UNDER THE ELECTRODES

- Leaving your TENS on for too long can result in over-stimulation. Allow the skin to heal and use TENS only for the periods described.

- Turning your TENS too high can cause skin problems. Allow the skin to heal and use TENS at a lower intensity.

- Some people experience an allergic reaction to the adhesive coating on the surface of the electrodes. Try using a different make of electrode if you suspect that this is the cause of the problem.

- If you continue to experience skin problems, you may try reducing the Pulse Width setting to 150 microseconds or even 100 microseconds if problems persist.
  This option is only effective if your pain is also reduced at the new lower setting.

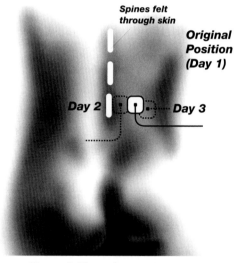

- Alternatively, move the electrode position each day by just the width of the electrode. You must ensure that the electrode is still positioned over the appropriate dermatome. (see *Figure 6*)

Figure 6. Electrode repositioning

- You may find it necessary to remove the electrodes after each treatment to allow the skin to recover.

ELECTRODES WON'T STICK

- **Oily skin.** Try thoroughly cleansing the skin with soap and water then rinse and dry the area well around the electrode sites. If this doesn't help, try cleansing the skin with a swab impregnated with alcohol. As a last resort, hold the electrode in place using a sticky tape such as Mircopore.

- **Hairy skin.** Clip away the hairs around the location of the electrode with scissors. Don't shave the area!

- **Perspiration.** The adhesive used on electrodes is water-based. If it becomes saturated, it will lose its adhesive qualities. Instead of placing the electrodes on the plastic film before going to bed, try leaving them face up overnight to allow them to dry out. Alternatively, equip yourself with two sets of electrodes and use one set for one day and the other the next.

- **Electrodes too dry.** As the electrode's adhesive is water-based, if they become too dry they can lose their adhesiveness. Before you go to bed, moisten the adhesive surface with just a few drops of water and place the moistened electrodes on the plastic backing overnight.

- **Wear and tear.** Eventually, your electrodes will wear out and require replacement. You can reasonably expect them to last for 4 to 12 weeks, depending on your skin type.

HEADACHES

TENS on certain settings will stimulate the production of endorphins and dynorphins. Even though these molecules have a role in reducing pain, they can sometimes cause a 'hangover' headache. If this can be avoided by changing the TENS settings to one of those previously described without affecting your pain management, continue with this course of action. If you are so sensitive to TENS that you suffer headaches on each of the alternative settings, you may reduce the Pulse Width control. Try 150 microseconds and if this does not help, reduce the Pulse Width to 100 microseconds. Again, this solution is only of value if your pain remains controlled on the new setting.

Central Neck Pain
Without Pain Radiating to the Arm

In each of the following ten examples, the radiated pain has been illustrated on the left side of the body, simply for the sake of clarity. If your radiated pain is on the right side of your body, the electrodes should be placed in a 'mirror image' of those shown here. Hold the picture up to a mirror and you will see clearly where to position your electrodes.

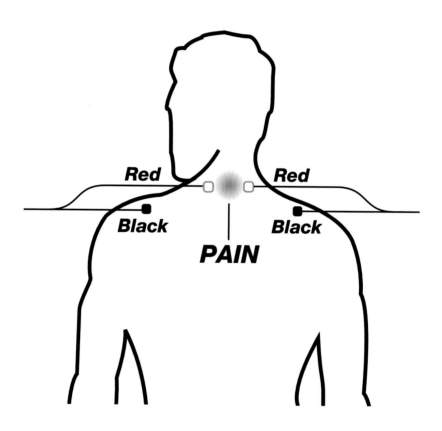

Central Neck Pain
With Pain Radiating to the Shoulder (*left shown*)

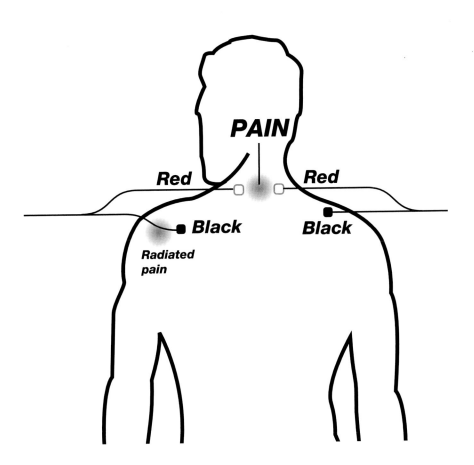

PAIN

Red

Red

Black

Black

Radiated
pain

Central Neck Pain

With Pain Radiating to the Back of the Arm (*left shown*)

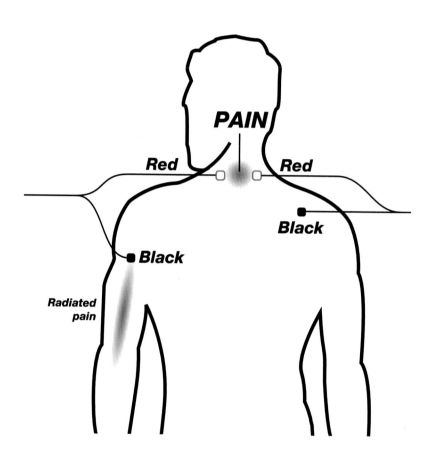

PAIN

Red

Red

Black

Black

Radiated pain

Central Neck Pain
With Pain Radiating to the Front of the Arm

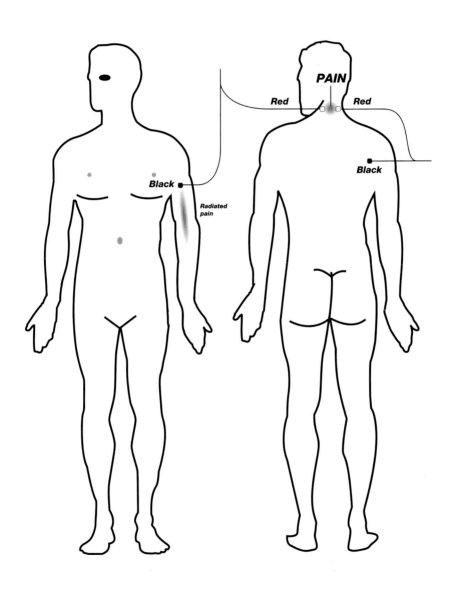

PAIN

Red

Red

Black

Black

Radiated pain

Shoulder Pain
Without Central Neck Pain

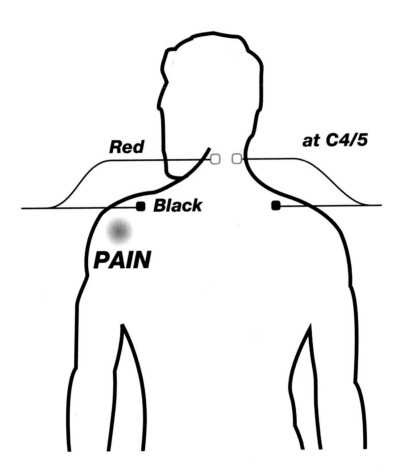

Red

at C4/5

Black

PAIN

Remember that TENS works by affecting the nerves and spinal cord. The red electrode is still placed alongside the spine.

Chest Wall Pain

due to i) injury, ii) post surgery, iii) post herpatic neuralgia (shingles)

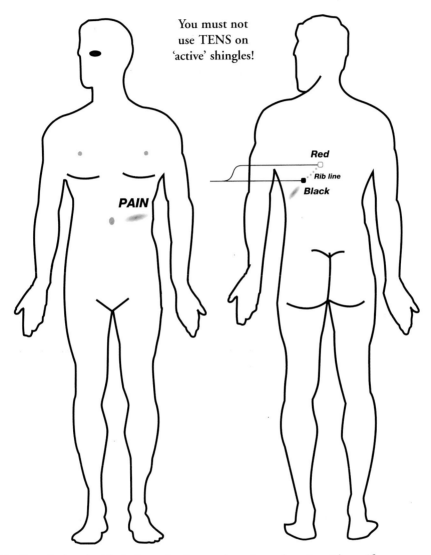

You must not use TENS on 'active' shingles!

PAIN

Red

Rib line

Black

Try first placing the black electrode close to the pain at the spine side, or if necessary, place it directly over the pain. Then follow the space between the ribs to the spine. Place the red electrode alongside the spine at that level.

Low Back Pain
Without Pain Radiating to other areas

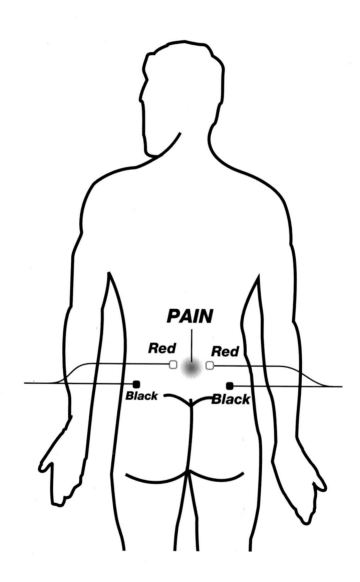

PAIN

Red   Red

Black   Black

Low Back Pain
With Pain Radiating to the Buttock

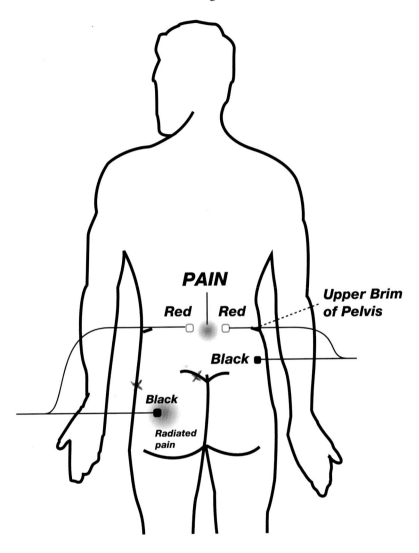

You may need to move the red electrode up or down a couple of vertebrae until you achieve good pain management.

Central Back Pain
With Pain Radiating to the Leg

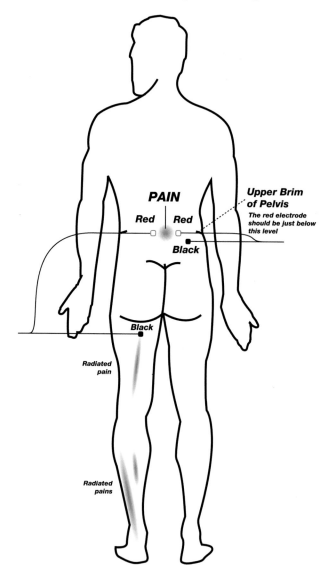

PAIN

Red | **Red**

Black

Upper Brim of Pelvis

The red electrode should be just below this level

Black

Radiated pain

Radiated pains

These electrode positions will also serve where pain is radiated to the back or side of the calf.

Low Back Pain
With Pain Radiating to the Front of the Leg

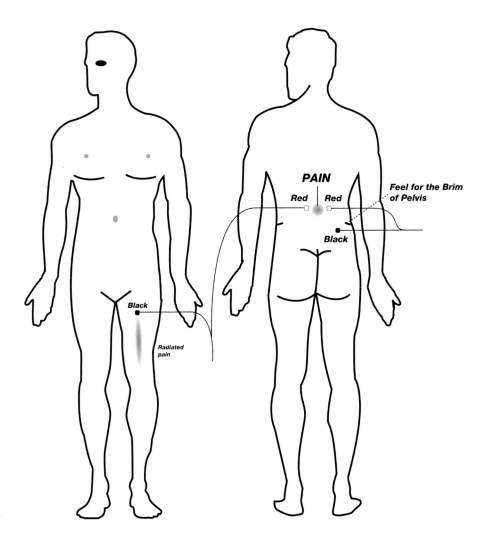

When pain is radiated to the front of the leg, L1, L2 or L3 may be the responsible level. You may find it necessary to move the red electrode up or down a vertebra to achieve good pain management.

Nausea

The causes of nausea can be varied and may be the result of an anaesthetic, certain medications or that seen in the early stages of pregnancy.
TENS can be used to treat nausea by placing the black electrodes over a very easily found acupuncture point. This point is called Circulation 6 and is described below.

If you turn your hand palm up you will notice that there are two or three skin creases where the wrist bends. Place the black electrode so that its centre is approximately two inches above the middle of the crease which is closest to the hand (see below).
The Red electrode may be placed over the same surface of the forearm - six inches higher or over the fleshy part of the hand just below the thumb.

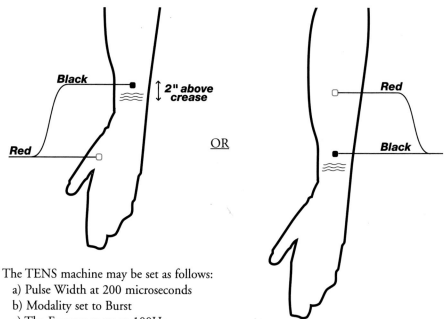

The TENS machine may be set as follows:
   a) Pulse Width at 200 microseconds
   b) Modality set to Burst
   c) The Frequency set to 100Hz
Stimulate for between five minutes and one hour. Repeat as often as necessary to control the nausea. Try to leave at least one hour between treatments.

If the above settings do not help, try the following:
   a) Pulse Width at 200 microseconds
   b) Modality set to Constant
   c) The Frequency set to 10-15Hz
Stimulate for five minutes every two hours.

Migraine and Headaches

There are several acupunture points that are used by clinicians to treat migraine. There is one which is easily located and often produces positive effects when stimulated with TENS. The point is called Colon 4 and is located on the hand (see below).
If you allow the thumb to lie against the hand, the soft tissue on the back of the hand between the base of the index finger and the wrist rises. The highest point of this 'mound' is Colon 4.
If you place your thumb from the other hand over this high point and then press firmly, you will find that this point is often tender to deep pressure just before, during and after headaches or migraine. This is the point over which you must place the black electrode. Place the electrodes on the side that displays the greatest degree of tenderness.

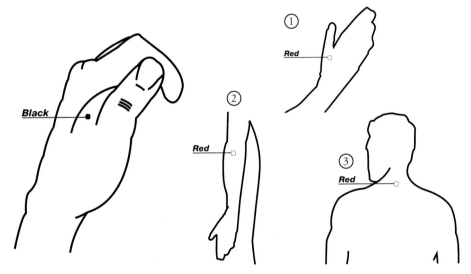

There are several sites where the red electrode may be placed.
Try each to discover which works best for you.
1) On the palm of the hand there is a fleshy pad at the base of the thumb
2) On the back of the forearm just below the elbow on the highest point of the muscle
3) Alongside the spine adjacent to the vertebra C6 on the same side as the black electrode
Set the TENS to Burst, 100Hz with a Pulse Width of 200 microseconds. Stimulate for up to one and a half hours. Repeat up to four times daily. If this is not successful, try Constant, 80-100Hz.
Stimulating one side only, often is sufficient to effect the pain. However, if a significant result is not evident, try stimulating both left and right sides.

Conclusion

Each individual may require different placements for electrodes. The positions shown in this book may provide a good starting point. There may also be an occasion when positioning the electrodes each side of a painful joint can help e.g. the front and back of a painful shoulder (see below).

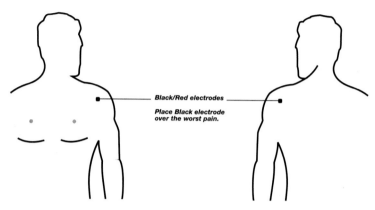

Black/Red electrodes

Place Black electrode over the worst pain.

Research has shown that the direct stimulation of nerves (that have been surgically exposed) with the red lead or anode can cause blocking of the nerve impluses under the electrode. This may not be the case when surface electrodes are used. However, if you find that you are not achieving good results with the electrode positions previously described, try moving the red electrode or simply reverse the lead wires. You must remember that the black electrode is the active electrode and therefore this should lie over one of the nerve bundles serving the painful area.

Following the instructions included in this book will provide you with a good foundation for pain management with TENS. You may need to 'fine tune' the position of the electrodes as each major nerve has contributions from several nerve roots. Happily, these are grouped together so moving the red electrode up and down a vertebra will suffice. You might also consider placing electrodes over the appropriate acupuncture points if you have followed the instructions yet failed to reduce your pain (see "King's Non-Invasive Acupuncture for everyone").

The subject covered by this book is fascinating but if all of the available information had been included, the book would have been far too unwieldy. Do work through all the alternatives before deciding that TENS is not helping. In the clinic where the author practiced, there were many cases where pain management was not achieved until the last combinations were tried, so persevere with your machine and stick by your routine to make the most of TENS.

Alan King